TRADITIONAL HOME BAKING

TRADITIONAL HOME BAKING

Marshall Cavendish

Editor: *Mary Devine*
Designer: *Johnny Pau*

Published by Marshall Cavendish Books Limited
58 Old Compton Street
London W1V 5PA

© Marshall Cavendish Limited 1986

Printed and bound in Hong Kong
by Dai Nippon Printing Company

ISBN 0 86307 425 1

INTRODUCTION

Few things are as welcoming or appetising as the delicious aroma of freshly baked cakes and bread, and there is something very satisfying about slicing into a crusty loaf or moist fruit cake that you have baked yourself. Although home baking requires a little time and effort, the rewards make it well worthwhile as everyone always appreciates home-made rather than shop-bought bakes. And thanks to modern mixers, freezers and microwave ovens, baking at home need not be a chore. Rather than baking every day, you can batch-bake when convenient, freeze the loaves or cakes, then simply pop them in the oven when needed.

If you have never tried home baking before, you will find our guide to baking techniques very useful. Step-by-step photographs illustrate baking methods and show you how to get the very best results. Then *Traditional Home Baking* presents a mouthwatering variety of easy recipes that include something special for practically every occasion.

Our cakes range from sumptuous, creamy gateaux – glamorous enough to serve at dinner parties – to simple, light sponges that round off afternoon tea perfectly. There are lots of plain or fancy biscuits that have plenty of 'child appeal', and melt-in-the-mouth pastries and pies – a really special treat.

Sometimes the simplest fare is the most delicious, so our bread recipes include plain loaves as well as fancy teabreads. Try our sweet or savoury scones too – they are just right for either breakfast or teatime.

All the recipes in *Traditional Home Baking* are so easy to follow that even complete beginners will soon feel confident enough to tackle the fanciest loaf or cake. And each recipe is shown in full colour so you can see just how good it will look on your table. A useful panel of Cook's Notes on every page provides all sorts of baking information, from cooking times and buying guides to freezing and storage advice, plus calorie counts for the weight watchers.

It's so easy to provide delicious home bakes that it's fun to take a break from everyday cooking and revive the delights of traditional home baking.

SYMBOLS

 TIME
Timing explained including preparation in advance

 SUPERQUICK
Dishes that are cooked within 1 hour

 FREEZING
The essential guide to dishes which freeze

 ECONOMY
Tips to make dishes go further, or for inexpensive ingredients

 WATCHPOINT
Look out for special advice on tricky methods

 DID YOU KNOW
Useful background to recipes or ingredients

 PREPARATION
Tips for techniques, often with illustrations

 SERVING IDEAS
Suggestions for good accompaniments

 SPECIAL OCCASIONS
Ideas to lift a dish out of the ordinary

 VARIATIONS
How to ring the changes on the basic dish

 COOK'S TIPS
Background information to help when you need it

 BUYING GUIDE
Guide to selecting suitable ingredients

 FOR CHILDREN
Adapting dishes for children's tastes

 STORAGE
How to store and for how long

CONTENTS

BREAD

Baking your own bread at home is very satisfying, and much less complicated than it seems at first sight. The following pages include all the basic information you need for bread-making, including how to use yeast and step-by-step instructions covering every stage of the operation.

MAKING AND BAKING BREAD DOUGH

Most household bread is made by the traditional method which is the double-rise method.

Mixing entails sifting the flour and salt into a warmed bowl. (Tip bran sifted out of wholemeal or wheatmeal flour into the bowl and stir it in.) Prepare the yeast as required and add to the flour. Add the liquid all at once and mix to a soft, slightly sticky dough with a wooden spoon or fork, or the fingers of one hand. If the dough feels too wet, work in a little extra flour but avoid making it too dry.

Kneading means vigorously pulling and stretching the dough; it strengthens the gluten in the flour, ensuring a good rise and an even texture.

Form the dough into a ball and turn it out on to a lightly floured surface. Lightly flour

your hands. Hold the edge nearest you steady with one hand; place the heel of the other hand in the centre and push down and away from you, stretching out the

Stretching the dough.

Folding it back to the centre.

dough. Fold the dough back to the centre and then give it a quarter turn. Continue stretching, folding and turning the dough for about 10 minutes until the dough feels

firm and elastic and is no longer sticky.

Mixing and kneading can be done using an electric table mixer with a dough hook attachment; follow the manufacturer's instructions.

Rising allows the yeast to do its work. Place the kneaded dough in an oiled large mixing bowl, cover with oiled polythene to prevent the surface drying out and cracking and leave to rise until doubled in bulk. The time depends on the temperature (see chart on following page). When ready, the dough should spring back if lightly pressed. If you refrigerate the dough, brush the surface with vegetable oil before covering.

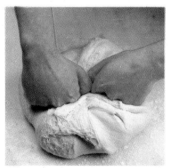

Knocking back is the term for punching air bubbles out of the risen dough. Turn the dough out on to a lightly floured surface and knead it vigorously with your knuck-

les for about 1 minute.

Proving is the word used for the second rising. Shape the dough, place it in an oiled tin, cover with oiled polythene and leave to rise until doubled in bulk. If you prove the dough in the refrigerator, let it come to room temperature before baking.

Glazing gives a crisp crust. Brush the top of the risen dough with salted water.

Baking: the dough is put into a very hot oven (220-230C/425-450F/Gas 7-8) to quickly kill the yeast and stop it raising the dough.

To test that the bread is done, turn it out of the tin and rap the underside smartly with your knuckles—it should sound hollow. If not, return the bread on its side to the oven and bake for a few minutes longer. Cool the baked bread on a wire rack before serving.

BREAD

INGREDIENTS

Strong plain flour, that is often sold as 'bread flour', is best In an emergency, ordinary (soft) plain flour will do, but the bread will be less well risen and will have both a closer texture and a much harder crust.

Strong white flour produces soft, spongy bread; wholemeal flour gives heavier, more chewy results. For a wholesome but light loaf, use wheatmeal flour or half strong white and half wholemeal flour.

Salt flavours the bread and helps to keep it moist. Measure the salt accurately—too much produces a hard crust—and sift it with the flour so that it is evenly blended.

Yeast raises the dough. Use fresh or dried yeast, whichever is more convenient. Generally, to raise a plain bread dough made with 750 g/1½ lb strong flour, use 15 g/½ oz fresh yeast, ½ tablespoon granular dried yeast, or a 7 g/¼ oz sachet easy-blend dried yeast.

Fat is not essential, but a small amount of lard, margarine, butter or vegetable oil will give a softer, moister texture.

Rising times for basic bread dough	
Warm place	45-60 minutes
Room temperature (18-21C/65-70F)	1½-2 hours
Cold room or larder	8-12 hours
Refrigerator	12-24 hours

The fat is rubbed into the sifted flour, oil is added with the liquid.

Liquid: this is generally water, but milk or a mixture of milk and water can be used for a softer result. The liquid should be tepid or 'hand hot' (43C/100F); hotter liquid will kill the yeast. As a guide, 450 g/1 lb strong white flour will absorb 300 ml/½ pint liquid; wholemeal and wheatmeal flours absorb slightly more.

PREPARING YEAST

Blend fresh yeast to a smooth, thin paste with a little of the tepid liquid from the quantity given in the recipe.

Granular dried yeast must be reconstituted before use: measure one-third of the tepid liquid specified in the recipe into a bowl and stir in ½ teaspoon sugar; sprinkle in the yeast and leave in a warm draught-free place for about 15 minutes until a frothy head has formed.

Easy-blend dried yeast needs no preparation: add it directly to the sifted flour.

BASIC WHITE BREAD

Makes 1 large loaf
750 g/1½ lb strong white flour
1½ teaspoons salt
15 g/½ oz margarine or butter
7 g/¼ oz sachet easy-blend dried yeast
450 ml/¾ pint tepid water
extra flour
vegetable oil, for greasing

1 Sift the flour and salt into a warmed large bowl. Rub in the fat, then stir in the yeast until well blended.

2 Pour in the tepid water and mix to a soft, slightly sticky dough which leaves the sides of the bowl cleanly. If the dough is too wet, work in a little extra flour.

3 Turn the dough out on to a lightly floured surface and knead vigorously for about 10 minutes until smooth and elastic and no longer sticky.

4 Shape the dough into a ball and place it in an oiled large bowl. Cover with oiled polythene and leave to rise until doubled in bulk (for exact time see chart).

5 Turn the dough out on to a lightly floured surface and knock back and knead with your knuckles for 1 minute.

6 Oil a 1 kg/2 lb loaf tin. Flatten the dough into an oblong about 38 × 23 cm/15 × 9 inches; fold it in 3 to make an oblong 23 × 13 cm/9 × 5 inches and fold the short ends inwards. Place seam-side down in the oiled tin.

7 Cover the tin with oiled polythene. Leave the dough to prove until it has almost reached the top of the tin.

8 Meanwhile, heat the oven to 230C/450F/Gas 8.

9 Bake the dough in the oven for 30-40 minutes until the bread is golden and just shrinking from the sides of the tin. Turn out the bread and rap the underside with your knuckles—if cooked it should sound hollow. If not cooked return the bread, on its side, to the oven and bake a few minutes longer. Cool on a wire rack.

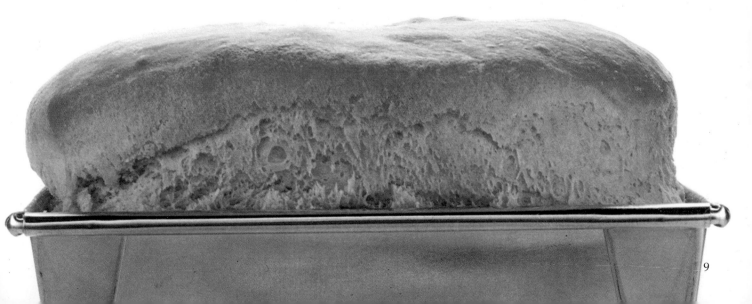

SHAPING BREAD DOUGH

When baking bread, it is fun to experiment and make loaves and rolls in a whole variety of different shapes and sizes, using a basic white bread dough, your favourite recipe or a packet mix. After shaping, bake the dough in oiled tins, on an oiled baking sheet or in an earthenware pot.

Bread dough should always be shaped after the first rise, and following knocking back. After shaping, cover with oiled polythene and allow to prove before baking.

BAKING LOAVES

Bake large loaves at a temperature of 230C/450F/Gas 8 for 30-40 minutes. If making a cottage loaf, reduce the oven temperature to 200C/400F/Gas 6 after the first 20 minutes, then continue baking for a further 25-35 minutes.

Tin loaf: flatten the dough out to an oblong about 2.5 cm/1 inch thick; fold it in 3 and fold the ends over the seam. Place seam-side-down in an oiled loaf tin; cover and prove.

Split tin: shape the dough as above; cover and prove for 10 minutes, make a deep cut lengthways down the centre, then finish proving.

Cob: knead the dough into a ball by drawing the sides upwards and into the centre. Place upside down on an oiled floured baking sheet with the tucks underneath. Cover and prove.

Latticed cob: shape dough as above, cover and prove until almost doubled in size. Sift a little flour over the top of the dough. Make several diagonal cuts, 2.5 cm/1 inch apart, across the top, then make another series of cuts, across the first set, to make a lattice pattern. Cover and prove for a further 10 minutes.

Crown loaf: divide the dough into 12 equal pieces and knead each into a ball. Place them slightly apart in an oiled large shallow round tin: make a ring with 9 of the balls around the sides of the tin and place remaining balls in centre. Cover and prove.

Plait: divide the dough into 3 equal pieces.

Roll each piece of dough into a long strand using the palms of your hands.

Starting at the centre, plait the strands loosely together down to one end. Dampen the end of each strand and pinch together.

Turn the dough over and around and plait from the centre to the other end; seal the ends. Place on an oiled baking sheet, cover and prove.

Cottage loaf: cut off one-third of the dough. Knead each piece into a round ball shape. Place the larger round on an oiled, floured baking sheet; slightly flatten the top.

Place the smaller round, well apart from the first, on the sheet. Cover and prove until almost doubled in size. With a sharp knife, cut a cross in the centre of the large round and dampen with water. Using a pastry brush, brush the underside of the small round with water to dampen it and place on top of large round, in centre.

Push the floured handle of a wooden spoon right through the centre of both rounds. If you wish, scissor snip around the edge of the top round (to give a notched effect) before baking.

SHAPING BREAD DOUGH

BAKING ROLLS

Bake rolls at a temperature of 230C/450F/Gas 8 for 15-20 minutes.

Round rolls: divide the dough into 50 g/2 oz pieces. On a lightly floured surface, roll each piece into a ball using the palm of one hand.

Still rolling the dough, gently press your hand down and immediately ease it up, cupping your fingers around the dough. Cover and prove.

Cloverleaf rolls: divide the dough into equal-sized pieces and roll into balls.

Place in groups of 3 in greased Yorkshire pudding or muffin tins; cover and prove.

Finger rolls: divide the dough into 50 g/2 oz pieces; roll into sausage shapes about 6.5 cm/2½ inches long. Place close together on an oiled baking sheet for soft sides, or 4 cm/1½ inches apart for crisper sides. Cover and prove.

BREAD/Variations

Basic white bread can be given extra interest and flavour simply by adding ingredients such as herbs, spices and dried fruit to the dough. Or you can try your hand at making a rich, sweet bread that would be a real tea-time treat for family and friends.

BREAD VARIATIONS

A basic loaf can be made richer and more interesting by the addition of a whole variety of ingredients. Ring the changes on a loaf made with 750 g/1½ lb flour in some of the following ways:

Herb bread (1): add 6 teaspoons of any mixture of dried herbs (or double the quantity of fresh herbs) to the dry ingredients. Try 2 teaspoons each marjoram, basil and thyme, or 2 teaspoons each rosemary, dill and sage.

Savoury seed bread (2): add to the dry ingredients 2 teaspoons each celery seeds, dill seeds and caraway seeds. Sprinkle one sort of seeds on top of the loaf before baking.

Savoury spiced rolls (3): add 2 teaspoons sweet paprika, 1 teaspoon ground coriander and ¼ teaspoon freshly ground black pepper to the dry ingredients.

Sweet spiced loaf (4): add 2 teaspoons mixed spice, plus 50 g/2 oz caster sugar to the dry ingredients. Fruit and/or nuts may be added, as below.

Fruit loaf (5): after the dough has risen for the first time, knead in 225 g/8 oz mixed dried fruit, or the same weight of currants, sultanas, raisins, chopped dates or cooked, chopped dried apricots or prunes. You can also use 100 g/4 oz chopped mixed peel or glacé cherries in place of half the fruit. The fruit may also be added to a rich, sweet bread (see below).

Rich sweet bread (5): for every 750 g/1½ lb flour stir in 75 g/3 oz caster sugar, then run in an extra 75 g/3 oz margarine or butter. Make up the liquid for the bread using half milk and half water, then continue in the usual way. For an even richer loaf, add 2 beaten eggs in place of 6 tablespoons of recipe liquid.

The soft dough of breads such as this is rather sticky, and so needs careful handling. It should be pounded and slapped rather than kneaded to keep it soft and pliable. Allow extra time for the dough to rise and bake it at 200C/400F/Gas 6.

The loaf may be varied by the addition of spices (but no more sugar), fruit or nuts, as above. The finished loaf may be glazed, or iced with a soft water icing.

GUIDE TO CAKE MAKING

Homemade cakes are always popular but, as every cook knows, they can be difficult to bake successfully. Follow our collection of tips to help avoid disaster, and use our clever suggestions for covering up catastrophes if they do occur. The following guide also tells you how to store cakes.

To save last-minute panic, follow this set of basic rules for cake making.

Before you begin

1 Read through the recipe at least once.
2 Assemble all the equipment and prepare the tin so that there is no delay between mixing and baking. Some recipes call for the tin to be oiled, others need to be oiled and then lined with grease-proof paper and oiled again.
3 Weigh and measure ingredients accurately so that the balance of the recipe is not upset. If necessary, remove eggs from the refrigerator for 1-2 hours so that they can come to room temperature.
4 Heat the oven to the recommended temperature.

During cake making

1 Put the cake into the pre-heated oven as soon as possible after it has been mixed.
2 Test a cake for doneness at the end of the minimum recommended baking time. If you open the oven door too early, before the cake is set, the sudden draught of cold air may make it sink. Test cakes as follows:

Small cakes/shallow sponges: press the top lightly at the centre. It should feel springy and leave no impression when you lift your fingertips.
Large, deep cakes: check that

the cake is just shrinking from the sides of the tin, then insert a warmed fine skewer into the centre. If the cake is done, the skewer should come out clean with no uncooked mixture clinging to it.
Rich fruit cakes: use the skewer test and also lift the cake close to your ear. A continuous sizzling sound means that it is not yet cooked.

Cooling

To make turning out as easy as possible, leave the cooked cake in the tin for a few minutes so that it can shrink slightly from the tin. Leave whisked sponges 1 minute; large cakes 3-5 minutes; rich fruit cakes 15-20 minutes. If a cake shows signs of sticking, run a palette knife around the sides of the tin to loosen it.

After turning out the cake, peel off the lining paper, turn the cake the right way up and leave it on a wire rack to cool so that air can circulate freely. This will prevent it from becoming soggy.

STORAGE

Many cakes will keep well if properly stored according to the following rules:
1 Do not store a cake until it is completely cold, or condensation will make it soggy.
2 Keep cakes which are filled and/or decorated with cream in the refrigerator.
3 Keep all other cakes in an airtight container with a well-fitting lid in a cool place. A

piece of apple in the container with an unwrapped cake will help keep the cake moist.
4 Wrap rich fruit cakes in cling film or foil before storing.
5 Never store cakes in the same container as biscuits—the biscuits will soften.

Storage times

Cakes stored according to the above rules should keep as follows:
Fatless whisked sponges: best eaten the same day, but may keep overnight.
Plain, rubbed in mixtures: 1-2 days.
Genoese sponges: 2-3 days.
Quick-mix cakes, made with soft margarine: 3-4 days.
Victoria sandwiches and other creamed cakes: 5-7 days.
Gingerbreads: up to 2 weeks.
Rich fruit cakes: several months.

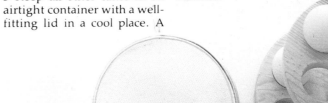

DEALING WITH DISASTERS

DEALING WITH DISASTERS

If your cake has not turned out as it should, you may at least be able to serve it as a dessert. Use the chart to identify the possible causes of the problem, then try one or more of the following remedies:

Dry, crumbly texture: return the cake to its tin and warm through in the oven, then prick the top all over with a fine skewer. Heat the syrup from a can of fruit and pour it over the warmed cake. Serve topped with drained fruit.

Coarse texture, with holes: crumble the cake and mix in enough milk and egg to give a dropping consistency. Bake in a 180C/350F/Gas 4 oven, or steam over boiling water until set. Serve hot, with pouring cream or custard.

Top hard and crusty: rub the fine holes of a grater over the surface. Brush off any loose crumbs, then dredge with icing sugar.

WHAT WENT WRONG

Close, heavy texture
- Too much liquid
- Too little raising agent
- Fat and sugar not beaten together thoroughly
- Mixture curdled when egg was added
- Flour stirred or beaten into mixture, not folded in
- Cake stored warm

Dry, crumbly texture
- Too much raising agent
- Cake overbaked in a cool oven

Burnt fruit
- Oven too hot
- Cake not covered with greaseproof paper after it started to colour

Coarse texture, with holes
- Cake overmixed when flour was added
- Mixture put into tin a little at a time so that pockets of air trapped in it

Pale and flat
- Tin too large (mixture cooks more quickly and so does not rise so well)

Sunken fruit
- Fruit damp or sticky (it must be rinsed and dried before use)
- Mixture too soft to support weight of fruit
- Too much raising agent (mixtures rises too fast to take fruit with it)

Cake sunk in centre
- Mixture too soft
- Too much raising agent (mixture rises high, then sinks)
- Oven too cool (cake does not cook through)
- Oven too hot (top cooked but centre still wet)
- Oven door opened before cake was set

Peaked or cracked on top
- Tin too small
- Mixture too stiff
- Oven too hot
- Cake placed too high in oven

Cake overflows
- Tin too small

Fruit sunk to the bottom: cut the cake in half horizontally to make 2 shallow cakes, one plain, one fruit. Serve each separately with the cut side underneath (the plain one may be iced).

Top peaked or badly cracked: trim the cake level, turn it over, then cover with buttercream and decorate.

Sunk in centre: cut out and remove the centre to make a ring cake. Ice and decorate, then fill with fruit.

BREAD

Cheese, celery and peanut loaf

MAKES 12 SLICES

280 g/10 oz packet brown bread
   mix
¼ teaspoon salt
pinch of freshly ground black
   pepper
1 teaspoon mustard powder
1 celery stalk, very finely chopped
50 g/2 oz mature Cheddar cheese,
   finely grated
185 ml/6½ fl oz tepid water
little beaten egg, for glazing
1 tablespoon chopped salted
   peanuts
vegetable oil, for greasing

1 Grease base and sides of a loaf tin: 6 cm/2¼ inches deep and about 20 × 10 cm/8 × 4 inches across the top. Set aside in a warm place (see Cook's tips).
2 Place the bread mix in a bowl and stir in the salt, pepper, mustard, celery and cheese. Add the water and mix to a dough.
3 Turn the dough out on to a floured surface and knead for 5 minutes, then place in the prepared tin and press gently to fit the shape. Cover the tin with oiled polythene and leave in a warm place for about 1¼ hours, or until the dough is risen and doubled in bulk.
4 Heat the oven to 200C/400F/Gas 6.
5 Uncover the loaf and brush the top with beaten egg, then sprinkle with the chopped peanuts. Bake in the oven for about 40 minutes, until cooked (see Cook's tips).
6 Place the loaf on a wire rack and leave to cool completely.

Cook's Notes

TIME
15 minutes preparation, 1¼ hours rising, 40 minutes baking plus cooling.

SERVING IDEAS
This loaf is best served fresh. It is delicious thickly sliced and buttered.

FREEZING
Wrap the cold loaf in a polythene bag, seal, label and freeze for up to 4 weeks. To serve: unwrap and defrost for 2-3 hours.

COOK'S TIPS
An airing cupboard is the ideal place to warm the tin and for the bread to rise. Keep the dough warm while mixing, kneading and rising: this ensures the yeast works fully and gives a springy texture.

To test that the loaf is cooked, turn it out of the tin and rap the underside with your knuckles: it should sound hollow. If not, return the loaf, on its side, to the oven and bake a little longer.

●100 calories/425 kj per slice

16

Apple currant plait

MAKES 10 SLICES
280 g/10 oz packet white bread mix
25 g/1 oz caster sugar
185 ml/6½ fl oz hand hot water
50 g/2 oz cooking apple, diced
50 g/2 oz currants
beaten egg, for glazing
crushed sugar lumps, to finish
vegetable oil, for greasing
butter, to serve

1 Put the bread mix into a bowl and stir in the sugar. Pour in the water and mix to a dough (see Cook's tips). Turn the dough out on to a floured surface, knead for 5 minutes, then work in the apple and currants (see Cook's tips).

2 Divide the dough into 3 equal pieces. Using your hands, roll each piece into a rope, about 38 cm/ 15 inches long. Lay ropes side-by-side on a work surface and plait them from the centre to one end, then from the centre to the other end to complete the plait.

3 Oil a large baking sheet. Place the loaf on the sheet and tuck the ends neatly underneath. Cover with oiled polythene and leave to rise in a warm place for about 1¼ hours, or until doubled in size.

4 About 20 minutes before the loaf is risen and doubled in size, heat the oven to 220C/425F/Gas 7.

5 Uncover the loaf and brush with beaten egg, then sprinkle with crushed sugar lumps. Bake in the oven for about 20 minutes, until risen and golden. Transfer to a wire rack and leave to cool completely. Serve sliced, with butter.

Cook's Notes

 TIME
2 hours preparation (including rising and baking), plus cooling time.

COOK'S TIPS
Keep the dough warm throughout mixing, kneading and rising: this ensures the yeast expands fully.
The fruit tends to stick to the outside of the dough: knead until it is incorporated.

 STORAGE
The loaf is best eaten on day of making, but any left over will keep for 2 days in a polythene bag.

●125 calories/525 kj per slice

17

Gingerbread

MAKES 16 SQUARES
175 g/6 oz margarine
200 g/7 oz golden syrup
150 g/5 oz black treacle
225 g/8 oz dark soft brown sugar
450 g/1 lb plain flour
1 tablespoon ground ginger
1 tablespoon baking powder
1 teaspoon bicarbonate of soda
1 teaspoon salt
1 egg, lightly beaten
300 ml/½ pint milk
melted margarine, for greasing

1 Heat the oven to 180C/350F/Gas 4. Grease a deep 23 cm/9 inch square cake tin with a loose base. Line the sides and base of the tin with greaseproof paper, then grease the paper.
2 Put the margarine, syrup, treacle and sugar into a heavy-based saucepan and heat gently, stirring, until the margarine has just melted. [!] Allow to cool slightly. [!]
3 Meanwhile, sift the flour, ginger, baking powder, bicarbonate of soda and salt into a large bowl, then make a well in the centre.
4 Add the egg, milk and melted mixture to the dry ingredients and mix with a wooden spoon until smoothly blended. Pour into the prepared tin and bake in the oven for about 1½ hours, until just firm to the touch.
5 Cool for 20 minutes, then remove from the tin and peel off the lining paper. Leave on a wire rack to cool completely. Wrap in foil and store in an airtight tin for 1 week before cutting (see Cook's tip).

Cook's Notes

TIME
10-15 minutes preparation, 1½ hours baking, plus cooling and storing time.

WATCHPOINTS
Keep the heat low and do not allow the mixture to boil or it will turn into toffee.
The melted mixture must be cooled a little, or it will cook the other ingredients slightly and toughen the cake.

COOK'S TIP
During storage the cake develops its characteristic moist and sticky texture, the flavour mellows and the crust softens. Gingerbread keeps well for 2-3 weeks. To serve: cut into 16 squares.

VARIATION
Store the cake for 1 week, then decorate the top with glacé icing made by blending 100 g/4 oz sifted icing sugar with 2-3 teaspoons water. Top with crystallized or drained stem ginger. Allow to set before cutting.

●315 calories/1325 kj per square

Syrup tea bread

MAKES 12-14 SLICES

350 g/12 oz plain flour
1 tablespoon baking powder
½ teaspoon bicarbonate of soda
50 g/2 oz stoned dates, chopped
50 g/2 oz seedless raisins
100 g/4 oz golden syrup
50 g/2 oz light soft brown sugar
300 ml/½ pint milk
50 g/2 oz margarine
vegetable oil, for greasing
butter, to serve

1 Heat the oven to 180C/350F/Gas 4. Grease a 1.75 L/3 pint (1 kg/2 lb) loaf tin, line the base with greaseproof paper, then grease the paper.
2 Sift the flour, baking powder and soda into a bowl, then stir in the chopped dates and raisins.
3 Put the syrup, sugar, milk and margarine into a heavy-based saucepan. Heat gently, stirring frequently with a wooden spoon, until the sugar has dissolved and the margarine has melted. ! Remove from the heat and pour on to the flour mixture, then beat with the spoon until the ingredients are evenly and thoroughly blended.
4 Spoon the mixture into the prepared tin and level the surface. Bake in oven for 1-1¼ hours, or until the bread is risen, well browned and firm to the touch. !
5 Cool the bread for 5 minutes, then run a palette knife around the sides to loosen it and turn out of the tin. Peel off the lining paper. Leave on a wire rack to cool completely (see Cook's tip). Serve sliced, with plenty of butter.

Cook's Notes

 TIME
20 minutes preparation, then 1-1¼ hours baking. Cooling takes about 1 hour.

 COOK'S TIP
The bread is ready for cutting as soon as it is cold. It is best served within 3 days of making.

 WATCHPOINTS
Do not let the syrup mixture become too hot or it will toughen the flour.
Check during baking and cover the bread with greaseproof paper, if necessary, to prevent the top overbrowning.

●215 calories/900 kj per slice

Currant bubble loaf

MAKES 16 SLICES

350 g/12 oz strong white flour
pinch of salt
75 g/3 oz butter, diced
100 g/4 oz caster sugar
7 g/¼ oz sachet easy-blend dried
   yeast
1 egg, beaten
125 ml/4 fl oz warm milk
1 teaspoon ground cinnamon
25 g/1 oz shelled walnuts, chopped
40 g/1½ oz currants
extra butter, for greasing

1 Sift the flour and salt into a large bowl. Rub in half the butter, then stir in half the sugar. Stir in the yeast. Make a well in the centre and pour in the egg.

2 Make the milk up to 175 ml/6 fl oz with hand-hot water, then pour into the well and mix to a dough. Turn out on to a lightly floured surface and knead for 10 minutes.

3 Clean and grease the bowl. Put dough into bowl and turn it over to lightly grease the surface. Cover with greased polythene; leave in a warm place for 1 hour, or until dough is doubled in bulk.

4 Gently melt remaining butter in a small pan, then remove from heat. In a small bowl, mix remaining sugar with the cinnamon and walnuts. Generously grease a 1.75 L/ 3 pint ring tin, then sprinkle in 4 teaspoons walnut mixture.

5 Turn the dough out on to a lightly floured surface and knead in the currants. Divide into 36 equal pieces and roll each into a ball.

6 Assemble loaf (see Preparation).

7 Cover and leave in a warm place for about 20 minutes, or until the dough has risen almost to the top of the tin. Meanwhile, heat the oven to 200C/400F/Gas 6.

8 Uncover the tin and bake above centre of oven for 10 minutes. Lower heat to 180C/350F/Gas 4 and bake for a further 20 minutes.

9. Cool loaf for 8-10 minutes. ⚠ Meanwhile, increase oven to 230C/ 450F/Gas 8. Turn loaf out on to a baking sheet. Return to oven for 4-5 minutes to brown top. Leave to cool, then invert on to a board.

20

Catherine-wheel spiced loaf

MAKES 10-12 SLICES

280 g/10 oz packet white bread mix
185 ml/6½ fl oz hand-hot water
3 tablespoons apricot jam
50 g/2 oz soft brown sugar
1 tablespoon ground cinnamon
milk, for brushing
vegetable oil, for greasing
butter, to serve

1 Place the bread mix in a bowl, then pour in the water and mix to a dough. Turn out the dough on to a floured surface and knead it for 5 minutes (see Cook's tips).

2 Roll out the dough to a rectangle, measuring about 35 × 15 cm/14 × 6 inches. Spread the jam over the surface, to within 1 cm/½ inch of the edges, then sprinkle over the sugar and cinnamon. Brush the edges of the dough with milk. Starting from 1 short end, carefully roll up the dough to enclose the spice mixture. Press the edges together to seal. !

3 Oil a 19 × 10 cm/7½ × 4 inch loaf tin. Place the roll in the oiled tin with the seal underneath. Cover with greased polythene and leave to rise in a warm place for about 1¼ hours or until doubled in size.

4 Heat the oven to 200C/400F/Gas 6.

5 Uncover the loaf and brush the top with milk. Bake in the oven for about 30 minutes, until well risen and golden brown. Cool the loaf in the tin for 10 minutes, then turn out on a wire rack and leave to cool completely. ✳ Store for 24 hours before cutting (see Cook's tips).

Cook's Notes

TIME
20 minutes preparation, then 1¼ hours rising and 30 minutes baking, plus cooling.

FREEZING
Seal the cold loaf in a polythene bag and freeze for up to 3 months. Defrost in wrappings at room temperature for 3-4 hours.

VARIATION
Omit the jam and cinnamon and use 3 tablespoons chunky marmalade and 1½ teaspoons ground ginger with the sugar.

COOK'S TIPS
Keep the dough warm to ensure the yeast expands it fully; this gives a springy texture to the loaf.

Store the loaf in a polythene bag or airtight tin for 24 hours before serving; if it is cut very fresh, the filling is a little sticky.

WATCHPOINT
It is essential to seal the edges of the dough securely to prevent the filling running out during baking.

●135 calories/575 kj per slice

Black olive bread

MAKES 10-12 SLICES

3 tablespoons olive oil
1 large onion, chopped
500 g/1 lb strong white flour
2 teaspoons salt
100 g/4 oz black olives, stoned and
    coarsely chopped (see
    Watchpoint)
2 teaspoons easy-blend dried yeast
200 ml/7 fl oz hand-hot water
6 whole black olives, stoned, to
    garnish (optional)
vegetable oil, for greasing

1 Heat 2 tablespoons oil in a pan, add the onion and fry gently for 5 minutes until soft and lightly coloured. Set aside to cool.
2 Sift the flour and salt into a warmed large bowl. Stir in the chopped olives, fried onion and any oil remaining in the pan. Stir in the yeast, mixing thoroughly, then make a well in the centre.
3 Pour in the warm water and mix to a dough. Turn the dough out on to a lightly floured surface and knead it for about 10 minutes, or until it is smooth and elastic.
4 Oil a baking sheet or tray.
5 Reserve one-third of the dough. Shape the remaining dough into a round, then gently press it out with the palm of your hand to a 20 cm/ 8 inch round. Place the round of dough on prepared baking sheet.
6 Shape remaining dough into a ball, then press it out to a 12.5 cm/ 5 inch round and place on top of larger round. Using a sharp knife, score a diamond pattern in the surface of the dough. Cover with oiled polythene and leave to rise in a warm place for 1-1½ hours, or until dough has doubled in size.
7 About 20 minutes before the dough is ready for baking, heat the oven to 220C/425F/Gas 7.
8 Uncover the dough and brush with the remaining olive oil. Press whole olives around the edge of the top round if liked. Bake the bread in the oven for 30-35 minutes until risen and golden brown. Cool completely on a wire rack before cutting.

Cook's Notes

TIME
25-30 minutes, plus about 1-1½ hours rising time and 30-35 minutes for baking the bread.

WATCHPOINT
If the olives are packed in brine, rinse them well and dry on absorbent paper or they will be too salty.

●225 calories/925 kj per slice

Savoury anchovy bread

MAKES 1 LARGE LOAF

500 g/1 lb 2 oz strong white flour
1 teaspoon salt
7 g/¼ oz sachet easy-blend dried
    yeast (see Cook's tip)
300 ml/11 fl oz tepid water
2 tablespoons olive oil
50 g/2 oz can anchovy fillets,
    drained and finely chopped
1 tablespoon tomato purée
beaten egg, to glaze
vegetable oil, for greasing

1 Sift the flour and salt into a warmed, large bowl. Stir in the yeast, then pour in the tepid water and the oil. Add the chopped anchovies and tomato purée. Using a wooden spoon and then your hands, mix to a soft dough.

2 Turn the dough out on to a lightly floured surface and then knead vigorously for about 10 minutes, until smooth and elastic and no longer sticky.

3 Shape the dough into a ball, place in an oiled, clean large bowl and cut a cross in the top. Cover with oiled polythene and leave to rise in a warm place for about 1 hour, or until doubled in bulk.

4 Heat the oven to 200C/400F/Gas 6. Oil a large baking sheet.

5 Turn the dough out on to a lightly floured surface and knead briefly with your knuckles. Roll out the dough to a round, about 23 cm/9 inches in diameter. Transfer to the prepared baking sheet and brush with beaten egg. Score the top with a sharp knife (see Preparation). Cover with oiled polythene or place in an oiled large polythene bag and leave to rise for 20 minutes.

6 Uncover and bake in the oven for 45 minutes, then turn the loaf over and bake upside down for 15 minutes more. Cool on a wire rack. To serve, break the bread apart into good-sized chunks.

Cook's Notes

TIME
2 hours preparation (including rising); 1 hour baking, plus cooling time.

COOK'S TIP
If you cannot obtain easy-blend yeast, use 1 tablespoon granular dried active baking yeast: dissolve ½ teaspoon sugar in one-third of the tepid water, sprinkle in the yeast and leave in a warm place for about 15 minutes until a frothy head forms; stir, then pour on to the sifted flour with the remaining tepid water.

STORAGE
Keep the bread in a polythene bag; it will stay fresh for 1-2 days.

PREPARATION
Chequerboard decoration makes an attractive finish; it also increases the area of crust.

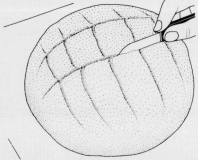

With a sharp knife, make several parallel cuts, 4 cm/1½ inches apart and 5 mm/¼ inch deep, across the surface of the dough. Make another series of parallel cuts at right angles to the first set, to give a chequerboard effect.

SERVING IDEAS
This bread has a soft, golden crust and a light, moist crumb. It is delicious with mild cheeses, as well as leafy green and vegetable salads. To serve the bread, do not cut it into slices with a knife, but break it into chunks with your hands.

●2140 calories/8950 kj per loaf

23

Malt fruit loaf

MAKES 8-10 SLICES

50 g/2 oz seedless raisins
50 g/2 oz sultanas
50 g/2 oz light soft brown sugar
100 g/4 oz wheat bran breakfast
  cereal (see Buying guide)
1 tablespoon malt extract (see
  Buying guide)
300 ml/½ pint milk
100 g/4 oz self-raising flour
extra malt extract, for glazing
vegetable oil, for greasing

1 Put the raisins, sultanas, sugar, cereal and malt into a large bowl. Pour in the milk and stir well to mix, then cover and leave in a cool place for 1 hour, stirring occasionally.

2 About 20 minutes before the end of standing time, heat the oven to 180C/350F/Gas 4. Very thoroughly grease an 850 ml/1½ pint (500 g/1 lb) loaf tin, line with greaseproof paper, then grease the paper.

3 Uncover the mixture, sift in the flour and mix with a wooden spoon until thoroughly blended. Turn the mixture into the prepared tin and bake in the oven for about 1 hour, until risen, browned and just firm to the touch.

4 Cool the loaf for 5 minutes, then run a palette knife around the sides to loosen it, turn out of the tin and carefully peel off the lining paper. Place the loaf on a wire rack and brush the top with malt extract, then leave to cool completely. Wrap and store in an airtight container for 24 hours before cutting.

Cook's Notes

TIME
2¾ hours preparation (including standing and baking), plus cooling and storing.

BUYING GUIDE
Look for an all-bran cereal—any natural high-fibre wheat bran cereal will do. Flakes, grains or strands are all suitable. Avoid those with added fruit or sweeteners.

Malt extract is a dark, sticky syrup derived from barley. It is sold in jars in chemists and health food shops, and keeps well in a cool, dark, dry place.

●170 calories/700 kj per slice

Wholemeal cheese baps

MAKES 8

450 g/1 lb wholemeal flour
1 teaspoon salt
2 teaspoons bicarbonate of soda
1 tablespoon sweet paprika
100 g/4 oz lard
200 g/7 oz Cheddar cheese, finely
   grated
300 ml/½ pint milk, soured with 2
   teaspoons lemon juice

1 Heat the oven to 200C/400F/Gas 6. Prepare a large baking sheet by sprinkling it with flour.
2 Sift the flour into a bowl with the salt, bicarbonate of soda and paprika, tipping in any bran left in the sieve.
3 Cut the lard into 5 mm/¼ inch cubes. Add to the flour and rub it in until the mixture is crumbly. Toss in two-thirds of the cheese and mix everything to a dough with the soured milk.
4 Divide the dough into 8 pieces. On a lightly floured surface, shape each one into a large, round, flat bap about 2 cm/¾ inch thick. Place them on the floured baking sheet.
5 Bake in the oven for 20 minutes. ✳ Take them out of the oven and put a portion of the remaining cheese on top of each. Return to the oven for 5 minutes.
6 Serve the baps while still warm, or let them cool on a wire rack.

Cook's Notes

TIME
Preparation 20 minutes.
Cooking 25 minutes.

FREEZING
To freeze:-cook the baps for the full 25 minutes without the cheese topping. Cool, seal, label and freeze. Store for up to 6 months. To serve: cook from frozen in an oven preheated to 200C/400F/Gas 6 for 10 minutes. Add the cheese topping and cook for another 5 minutes.

●360 calories/1500 kj per bap

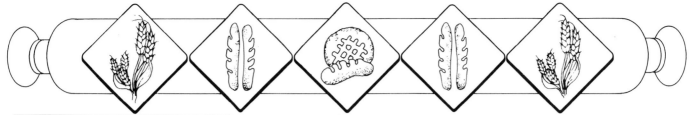

Plaited fruit loaf

MAKES 10 SLICES

280 g/10 oz packet white bread mix
¼ teaspoon ground ginger
185 ml/6½ fl oz tepid water
50 g/2 oz seedless raisins
50 g/2 oz cut mixed peel
beaten egg, for glazing
½ teaspoon poppy seeds (see Buying guide)
vegetable oil, for greasing

1 Place the bread mix in a bowl and stir in the ginger. Add the water and mix to a dough (see Cook's tips). Turn out on to a floured surface and knead for 5 minutes, then work in the raisins and peel (see Cook's tips).
2 Divide the dough into 3 equal pieces. Using your hands, roll each piece into a sausage shape, about 38 cm/15 inches long. Lay the rolls side by side and plait them from the centre to one end, then from the centre to the other end.
3 Oil a large baking sheet. Place the plaited loaf on the sheet and tuck the ends neatly underneath. Cover with oiled polythene and leave to rise in a warm place for about 1¼ hours, or until the loaf is doubled in bulk.
4 About 20 minutes before the loaf is risen, heat the oven to 220C/425F/ Gas 7.
5 Uncover the loaf, brush it with beaten egg, then sprinkle with the poppy seeds. Bake in the oven for about 20 minutes, until well risen and golden. Transfer to a wire rack and leave to cool completely before slicing and eating with butter.

Cook's Notes

TIME
2 hours (including rising and baking), plus cooling time.

COOK'S TIPS
Keep the dough warm throughout mixing, kneading and rising: this ensures the yeast expands fully and gives a springy texture to the loaf.
The fruit and peel tend to stick on the outside of the dough to begin with, so you need to persevere with kneading until they are well incorporated.

BUYING GUIDE
You can buy small quantities of poppy seeds in packets and small jars from health food stores, delicatessens and some supermarkets.

STORAGE
The loaf keeps fresh for up to 2 days if stored wrapped in a polythene bag.

● 130 calories/550 kj per slice

Onion bread

MAKES 8 WEDGES
280 g/10 oz packet white bread mix
200 ml/7 fl oz hand-hot water
50 g/2 oz margarine or butter
250 g/9 oz onions, thinly sliced
300 ml/½ pint soured cream
salt and freshly ground black pepper
1 teaspoon poppy seeds
vegetable oil, for greasing
flour, for dusting

1 Oil a 23 cm/9 inch sandwich cake tin or a Swiss roll tin, dust with flour and set aside in a warm place.
2 Put the bread mix into a bowl, add the water and mix to a fairly firm dough. Turn the dough out on to a lightly floured surface and knead for 5 minutes, until it is smooth and elastic (see Cook's tip).

3 Gently press the dough into the prepared cake tin, or make into a round on the Swiss roll tin. Cover with oiled polythene and leave in a warm place for 30-40 minutes, or until the dough has at least doubled in bulk.
4 Meanwhile, make the topping: melt the margarine in a saucepan and gently fry the onions for 5 minutes, until soft and lightly coloured. Remove pan from the heat and allow the onions to cool a little, then stir in the soured cream and salt and pepper to taste.
5 About 20 minutes before the dough is risen, heat the oven to 200C/400F/Gas 6.
6 Uncover the loaf and spread the onion mixture over the risen dough, then sprinkle the poppy seeds on top. Bake in the oven for 45-50 minutes, until the topping is set and lightly golden and the bread is cooked crisp at its edges.
7 Serve hot or cold, cut in wedges.

Pitta bread

MAKES 6

 280 g/10 oz sachet white bread mix
185 ml/6½ fl oz tepid water (see Watchpoints)
vegetable oil, for greasing and brushing

1 Place the bread mix in a bowl. Pour in the water, then mix to a dough with your hand or a wooden spoon. Turn the dough out on to a floured surface and knead for 5 minutes, until smooth and elastic.
2 Form the dough into a ball and place in an oiled, large bowl. Cover the bowl with oiled polythene or cling film and leave in a warm place for about 45 minutes, or until the dough is risen and doubled in size.
3 Turn the risen dough out on to a floured surface, knead for 1 minute, then divide into 6 equal pieces.
4 Heat the grill to high.
5 Roll out each piece of dough to an oval, measuring about 23 × 10 cm/ 9 × 4 inches. Arrange 3 of them on an inverted large baking tray. Brush the surface of each with oil, then grill for about 2 minutes, until coloured. Turn the pittas over and brush with oil, then return to the grill for a further 2 minutes.
6 Wrap the pittas in a clean tea-towel to keep them soft while you cook the remaining pittas in the same way. Serve warm.

Cook's Notes

TIME
20 minutes preparation; rising takes about 45 minutes and total cooking time is about 8 minutes.

WATCHPOINTS
Test the temperature of the water with a finger: it should feel comfortably warm. Do not use boiling hot water as this will kill the yeast.

Watch the pittas constantly during cooking and turn them around, as necessary, so they brown evenly.

● 165 calories/700 kj per pitta

Apricot and raisin teabread

MAKES 8 SLICES

280 g/10 oz packet white bread mix
25 g/1 oz caster sugar
½ teaspoon ground ginger
185 ml/6½ fl oz hand-hot water (see Preparation)
50 g/2 oz dried apricots, finely chopped
50 g/2 oz seedless raisins
2 teaspoons clear honey, to glaze
vegetable oil, for greasing

1 Brush the base and sides of an 850 ml/1½ pint (500 g/1 lb) loaf tin with oil; leave in a warm place.
2 Put the bread mix into a bowl and stir in the sugar and ginger. Add the water and mix to a dough. ⚠
3 Turn the dough out on to a floured work surface and knead for 5 minutes. Work in apricots and raisins, then place in the prepared tin and press gently to fit the shape.

Cook's Notes

⏰ TIME
15 minutes preparation, 1¼ hours rising, then 40 minutes baking plus cooling before serving.

PREPARATION
To create hand-hot water, mix half boiling and half cold water.

✳ FREEZING
Cool completely, then wrap, unglazed, in a polythene bag. Seal, label and freeze for up to 4 weeks. To serve: unwrap and defrost for 2-3 hours. Brush with honey before serving.

VARIATION
Add ½ teaspoon ground cinnamon instead of ginger to dry bread mix. Try substituting 50 g/2 oz chopped dried (not pressed) dates and 50 g/2 oz chopped walnuts for the dried apricots and seedless raisins.

❗ WATCHPOINT
Keep the dough warm throughout the mixing, kneading and rising processes to ensure the yeast expands the dough fully: this gives a springy texture to the baked loaf.

●165 calories/700 kj per slice

Cover the tin with oiled polythene and leave in a warm place for about 1¼ hours, or until the dough is risen and doubled in bulk.
4 Heat the oven to 200C/400F/Gas 6.
5 Uncover the loaf and bake for about 40 minutes, or until golden.
6 Leave the loaf in the tin for about 2 minutes, then turn out. Place the right way up on a wire rack. ✳Brush the honey over the crust to glaze, then leave to cool completely.

Lager loaf

MAKES 6-8 WEDGES

300 ml/½ pint lager
500 g/1 lb strong plain white flour

2 teaspoons salt
15 g/½ oz lard, cut into flakes
1 teaspoon dried rosemary
2 teaspoons easy-blend dried yeast
milk, for glazing
vegetable oil, for greasing

1 Pour the lager into a saucepan and heat gently until tepid (see Cook's tips). Remove from the heat and set aside. Oil a baking sheet.
2 Sift the flour and salt into a warmed, large bowl. Add the lard and rub it in with your fingertips, [!] then stir in the rosemary and yeast. Make a well in the centre.
3 Pour in the warmed lager and mix to a dough. Turn out on to a floured surface and knead for about 10 minutes, until smooth and elastic and no longer sticky.
4 Shape the dough into a round and

place on the prepared baking sheet. Using a sharp knife, score a cross on the top of the dough, about 10 cm/4 inches long and 1 cm/½ inch deep. Cover with oiled polythene and leave to rise in a warm place for 1½ hours, or until the dough has doubled in size.
5 About 15 minutes before the dough is ready, heat the oven to 220C/425F/Gas 7.
6 Uncover the dough and brush the top lightly with milk. Bake in the oven for 35-40 minutes, until risen and deep golden brown (see Cook's tips). Transfer to a wire rack and leave to cool completely.
7 To serve: cut the cold loaf across into thick slices or, if you wish, cut it into wedges like a cake (see Serving ideas).

Cook's Notes

 TIME
20 minutes preparation, 1½ hours rising and 35-40 minutes baking, plus cooling.

 COOK'S TIPS
Check the temperature of the lager with a clean finger: it should feel comfortably warm.
To test that the loaf is cooked, rap the underside with your knuckles: it should sound hollow. If not, return the loaf upside down to the oven and bake a little longer.

[!] **WATCHPOINT**
When using easy-blend dried yeast it is essential to rub in any fat used before adding the yeast to the dry ingredients, otherwise the dough will not rise.

 SERVING IDEAS
Serve this loaf with butter, a wedge of mature Cheddar cheese—and plenty of cold lager to drink.

● 335 calories/1400 kj per wedge

Country loaf

MAKES 16-18 SLICES
450 g/1 lb granary bread flour (see Did you know)
1 teaspoon salt
7 g/¼ oz sachet easy-blend dried yeast
300 ml/½ pint hand-hot water
extra granary flour, for dusting
vegetable oil, for greasing
butter, to serve

1 Brush a 1.7 L/3 pint (1 kg/2 lb) loaf tin thoroughly with oil, then set aside in a warm place.
2 Put the flour into a warmed large bowl and stir in the salt and yeast. Make a well in the centre, then pour in most of the water. Using a wooden spoon and then your hands, mix to a soft dough, adding the remaining water if the consistency of the dough is too stiff.
3 Turn the dough out on to a lightly floured surface and knead briefly until no longer sticky. Shape the dough into an oblong, then press it out with the heel of your hand until slightly longer and three times wider than the base of the tin.
4 Arrange dough so that the short ends face you. Fold the top third over the centre section, then bring the bottom third over the 2 layers. Turn the dough over, so the seam is underneath and tuck the ends under. Place the dough in the prepared tin, pressing it well into the corners to give a good shape.
5 Brush the top lightly with water, then sprinkle with flour. Cover with oiled polythene, or place in a large oiled polythene bag and leave to rise in a warm place for 30 minutes, until the dough reaches the top of the tin.
6 About 20 minutes before the dough is ready, heat the oven to 200C/400F/Gas 6.
7 Uncover loaf and bake in the oven for 40 minutes. Remove from the oven and run a palette knife around the sides, then turn out of tin.
8 Return loaf, upside down, to oven for a further 5-10 minutes to crisp the base and sides (see Cook's tip). Cool completely on a wire rack before cutting. Slice the loaf thickly and serve with butter.

Sticky figgy loaf

MAKES 8-10 SLICES

100 g/4 oz dried figs (see
    Watchpoints), coarsely chopped
50 g/2 oz Demerara sugar
100 g/4 oz wheat bran breakfast
    cereal (see Buying guide)
1 tablespoon clear honey
300 ml/½ pint milk
100 g/4 oz self-raising flour
vegetable oil, for greasing

1 Put the figs, sugar, cereal and
honey into a bowl. Pour over the
milk and stir to mix. Cover and
leave to stand in a cool place for
1 hour, stirring occasionally.
2 About 20 minutes before the end
of standing time, heat the oven to
180C/350F/Gas 4. Thoroughly oil an
850 ml/1½ pint (500 g/1 lb) loaf tin,
line the tin with greaseproof paper,

and then oil the greaseproof paper.
3 Uncover the figgy mixture. Sift in
the flour and mix thoroughly with a
wooden spoon. !
4 Turn the mixture into the prepared tin and bake in the oven for
1-1¼ hours, until risen, browned
and just firm to the touch. Cover
with greaseproof paper halfway
through baking to avoid the figgy

loaf overbrowning on the top.
5 Cool the loaf for 5 minutes, then
run a palette knife around the sides
to loosen it and turn out of the tin.
Peel off the lining paper. Leave the
loaf, right way up, on a wire rack to
cool completely. Wrap in foil or
cling film and store for 24 hours
before cutting into chunky slices
(see Cook's tip).

Cook's Notes

TIME
25 minutes preparation,
plus 1 hour standing
and 1-1¼ hours baking. Allow
time for cooling and storing.

WATCHPOINTS
Discard any hard stalks
from the figs as these
are unpleasant to eat.
  The ingredients must be well
mixed or streaks of flour will
spoil the look of the loaf.

BUYING GUIDE
Look for an all-bran
cereal – any high-fibre
wheat bran cereal will do.

COOK'S TIP
The loaf becomes moist
and sticky when stored.
It will keep for up to 1 week in
an airtight container. Serve with
butter or cheese.

●160 calories/650 kj per slice

Vienna rolls

MAKES 12

700 g/1½ lb strong white flour
2 teaspoons salt
25 g/1 oz lard, diced
7 g/¼ oz sachet easy-blend dried
   yeast
225 ml/8 fl oz warm milk
200 ml/7 fl oz hand-hot water
50 ml/2 fl oz single cream
   or high-cream milk, for glazing
poppy or caraway seeds (optional)
vegetable oil, for greasing

1 Sift the flour and salt into a warmed large bowl. Rub in lard then stir in the yeast. Make a well in the centre. Mix the milk with the water and pour into the well, then mix to a firm dough.

2 Turn the dough out on to a lightly floured surface and knead for 10 minutes until smooth and elastic, then form into a ball. Clean and grease the bowl. Return the dough to the bowl and turn it over to coat the surface lightly with oil. Cover the bowl with oiled polythene and leave to rise in a warm place for about 1 hour, or until the dough is doubled in bulk.

3 Grease 2 baking sheets or trays thoroughly with vegetable oil.

4 Turn the dough out on to a lightly floured surface and knead for 2 minutes, then shape into rolls and arrange on baking sheets (see Preparation). Cover with oiled polythene and leave to rise in a warm place for 30 minutes, or until doubled in size.

5 Meanwhile, heat the oven to 230C/450F/Gas 8. Place a roasting tin in bottom of oven and pour in enough boiling water to come half-way up sides (see Did you know).

6 Uncover the rolls and bake in centre and just above centre of oven for 10 minutes. Remove the tin of water. Allow steam to escape from oven. Brush top and sides of rolls with cream, then sprinkle with seeds, if using.

7 Return to the oven, swapping the sheets, for a further 10 minutes, or until the rolls are rich golden brown and shiny. Transfer to a wire rack and leave to cool completely. ✳

Cook's Notes

TIME
30 minutes preparation, 1½ hours rising, then 20 minutes baking, plus about 1 hour for cooling.

DID YOU KNOW
Creating a steamy atmosphere in the oven for the first half of baking time gives the rolls a soft crust.

FREEZING
Wrap in foil, then freeze for up to 4 months. Defrost in wrapping for 4 hours, then put in moderate oven for 10 minutes.

●255 calories/1075 kj per roll

PREPARATION
Keep bulk of dough covered while shaping each roll as follows:

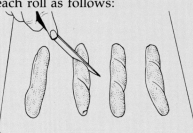

Divide the dough into 12 pieces, then roll out each to 15 × 7.5 cm/ 6 × 3 inch oval. Roll up tightly from 1 long side, then place seam side down on oiled baking sheet. Make 11 more rolls spacing well apart. Slash diagonally on top.

Irish soda bread

MAKES 24 SLICES
450 g/1 lb plain flour
1 teaspoon bicarbonate of soda
1 teaspoon salt
40 g/1½ oz butter or lard, diced
300-350 ml/10-12 fl oz plain
   buttermilk (see Cook's tip)
plain flour, for dusting

1 Heat the oven to 200C/400F/Gas 6. Sift a thin dusting of flour over a baking sheet.
2 Sift the flour, bicarbonate of soda and salt into a bowl, then rub in the butter. Make a well in the centre and pour in 300 ml/½ pint buttermilk. Mix quickly to a soft dough with a fork, adding more buttermilk if necessary.
3 With floured hands, gather the dough together, turn out on to a floured surface and knead lightly and briefly until smooth. Shape the dough into a round, about 18 cm/7 inches in diameter, then place on the prepared baking sheet.

Cook's Notes

 TIME
45 minutes preparation plus cooling time.

COOK'S TIP
If buttermilk is not available, use 300 ml/½ pint fresh milk and stir in 1 teaspoon cream of tartar. Add extra fresh milk, if necessary, when mixing the dough to give the right consistency.

 FREEZING
Wrap cold bread in polythene bag and freeze for up to 6 months. To serve: remove from bag, wrap in foil and reheat in a 200C/400F/Gas 6 oven. Allow 25 minutes for whole loaf; 15 minutes for a quarter section.

●85 calories/350 kj per slice

 SERVING IDEAS
Eat the bread warm, or as soon as it is cold. To serve, break apart (do not cut) into wedges, then slice thickly. Any left over can be frozen, or toasted.

 PREPARATION
To score the dough into quarters:

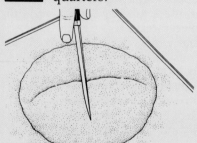

Cut a deep cross in the dough with a sharp, floured knife, to within 1 cm/½ inch of edges.

4 Score round into quarters (see Preparation). Bake the bread in the top of the oven for about 30 minutes, until golden brown and the under-side sounds hollow when rapped.
5 Transfer the bread to a wire rack, cover with a clean tea-towel and leave to cool (see Serving ideas).

Banana teabread

MAKES 12 SLICES

 225 g/8 oz self-raising flour
½ teaspoon ground mixed spice
 100 g/4 oz margarine, softened
100 g/4 oz light soft brown sugar
2 eggs
500 g/1 lb bananas, mashed (see
  Economy)
1 tablespoon Demerara sugar
vegetable oil, for greasing

1 Heat the oven to 180C/350F/Gas 4. Grease a 1.75 L/3 pint (1 kg/2 lb) loaf tin, line the base with greaseproof paper, then grease the paper.
2 Sift flour and spice into a bowl.
3 Beat the margarine and sugar until pale and fluffy, then beat in 1 egg. Add the remaining egg and 1 tablespoon of the flour mixture and beat vigorously until evenly blended (see Cook's tip). Beat in bananas.

4 Using a large metal spoon, fold in the remaining flour mixture. Spoon the mixture into the prepared tin and level the surface, then sprinkle over the Demerara sugar.
5 Bake in the oven for 1-1¼ hours, or until firm to the touch.

6 Cool the teabread for 1 minute, then run a palette knife around the sides to loosen it, turn out of tin and peel off lining paper. Turn right way up and leave on a wire rack to cool completely before slicing (see Serving ideas).

Cook's Notes

TIME
20 minutes preparation and 1-1¼ hours baking, plus cooling time.

STORAGE
The teabread will keep fresh for 3-4 days if wrapped in foil and stored in an airtight container.

FREEZING
Wrap in a polythene bag, seal, label and freeze for up to 6 months. To serve: defrost in wrapping at room temperature for 3 hours.

COOK'S TIP
A little flour prevents the mixture curdling when the second egg is added.

SERVING IDEAS
This teabread is moist enough to serve plain, but can be buttered. It is ideal for picnics.

ECONOMY
This tasty teabread is a good way to use up over-soft bananas.

● 195 calories/825 kj per slice

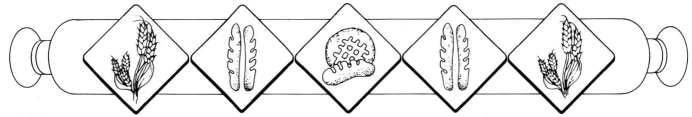

Mustard knots

MAKES 8
280 g/10 oz packet brown bread mix
1 teaspoon mustard powder
freshly ground black pepper
65 g/2½ oz Leicester cheese, grated
200 ml/7 fl oz hand-hot water
milk, for glazing
vegetable oil, for greasing
butter, to serve
slices of cheese (optional)

1 Place the bread mix in a bowl and stir in the mustard, a grinding of black pepper and 50 g/2 oz cheese. Pour in the water and mix to a dough. Turn out the dough on to a floured surface and knead it for 5 minutes.
2 Oil a large baking sheet.

3 Divide the dough into 8 equal pieces. Using your fingertips, roll each piece back and forth on the work surface to make a 'rope', about 30 cm/12 inches long. Shape each 'rope' of dough into a knot (see Preparation). Place the knots well apart on the prepared baking sheet. Cover with oiled polythene and leave to rise in a warm place for about 40 minutes, until they have doubled in size.
4 About 20 minutes before the dough is ready, heat the oven to 220C/425F/Gas 7.
5 Uncover the knots and brush each with milk, then sprinkle lightly with the remaining cheese. Bake in the oven for 25-30 minutes, until risen and golden. Transfer to a wire rack to cool. Serve the knots warm or cold, split in half and generously buttered, or filled with slices of cheese, if liked. Serve alone or with a soup or salad.

Cook's Notes

 TIME
1½ hours (including rising and baking), plus cooling time.

 PREPARATION
Shape the dough into knots as follows:

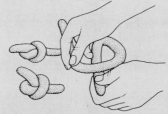

Make a loop (see above), 5 cm/2 inches from one end, then gently pull the longer end through the loop to make a knot.

●160 calories/650 kj per knot

36

CAKES

Pineapple and ginger cake

SERVES 6

125 g/4 oz self-raising flour
1 teaspoon baking powder
125 g/4 oz soft tub margarine
100 g/3½ oz caster sugar
2 large eggs
40 g/1½ oz drained stem ginger,
  finely chopped (see Buying
  guide)
melted margarine, for greasing

TOPPING
25 g/1 oz margarine
75 g/3 oz light soft brown sugar
225 g/8 oz can pineapple rings,
  drained
1 piece stem ginger, drained
angelica, cut into 'leaves'

1 Heat the oven to 170C/325F/Gas 3. Grease a deep 19-20 cm/7½-8 inch cake tin with melted margarine, then line the base with a circle of foil (see Cook's tip).

2 Make the topping: melt the margarine in a small pan, add the brown sugar and stir over gentle heat until the sugar has melted. Spread the mixture over the base of the tin.

3 Pat the pineapple rings dry with absorbent paper, then halve them and arrange on the sugar mixture in a decorative pattern. Slice the piece of stem ginger. Put one piece in the semi-circle of each halved pineapple ring and one in the middle. Arrange leaves of angelica around the edge and in the centre.

4 Make the cake: sift the flour and baking powder into a bowl. Add the margarine, caster sugar, eggs and chopped stem ginger and beat together with a wooden spoon for 2-3 minutes, until pale and fluffy. Spoon the mixture carefully into the tin and level surface with a spatula.

5 Bake in the oven for 70 minutes, until the cake is springy to the touch at the centre and is shrinking slightly from the sides of the tin.

6 Cool the cake in the tin for 5 minutes, then run a palette knife around the edge and turn out on to a wire rack. Carefully peel off the foil, leave to cool completely, then transfer to a serving plate. Serve as soon as possible (see Storage).

Cook's Notes

 TIME
30 minutes preparation, 70 minutes baking.

 VARIATIONS
Use halved glacé cherries for the decoration in place of the sliced ginger. If you wish, omit the chopped ginger from the cake mixture and increase the caster sugar to 125 g/4 oz.

 STORAGE
This cake will keep for up to 3 days in an airtight tin, but it is best served on the day it is made, because the topping soon loses its glossy appearance.

 **BUYING GUIDE**
Stem ginger in syrup is available in jars from delicatessens and many large supermarkets. It is fairly expensive, but you only need a little for this recipe.

 COOK'S TIP
If you only have a tin with a loose base, cut a circle of foil 2 cm/1 inch larger than the base of the tin and use this to line the base. Fold up the extra foil around the edge and press it against the sides, then brush the turned-up edges with melted margarine.

● 450 calories/1875 kj per portion

Orange cream sponge

MAKES 6-8 SLICES

3 large eggs
75 g/3 oz caster sugar
75 g/3 oz plain flour
vegetable oil, for greasing

FILLING AND DECORATION
150 ml/¼ pint double cream
1 tablespoon milk
5 tablespoons orange curd
6-8 orange twists (see Preparation)

1 Heat the oven to 190C/375F/Gas 5. Lightly grease two 18 cm/7 inch sandwich tins, line their bases with greaseproof paper, then lightly grease the paper.

2 Put the eggs and sugar into a heatproof bowl. Set the bowl over a pan of gently simmering water (see Cook's tip). Using a rotary or hand-held electric whisk, beat until the mixture is thick enough to hold the trail of the whisk for 3 seconds when the beaters are lifted.

3 Remove the bowl from the pan and whisk for a few minutes more, until the mixture is cool. Sift one-third of the flour over the mixture, then fold it in with a large metal spoon. Add the remaining flour in the same way.

4 Divide the mixture equally between the prepared tins and spread it evenly by gently tilting the tins. Bake immediately in the oven for 15 minutes, until the cakes are golden and springy to the touch.

5 Cool for 1-2 seconds, then turn out of the tins on to a wire rack. Peel off the lining paper and leave to cool completely.

6 To serve: whip the cream with the milk until standing in soft peaks, then fold in the orange curd. Place 1 cake on a serving plate and spread with some of the orange cream. Place the other cake on top. Spread the remaining orange cream over the top and sides of the cake, covering it completely. Decorate with orange twists and serve as soon as possible.

Cook's Notes

TIME
The sponge takes a total of 1¼-1½ hours to make.

PREPARATION
Make the orange twists as follows:

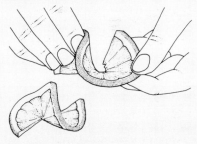

Cut 3 or 4 thin slices of orange. Remove any pips with the point of the knife. Make 1 cut from the centre to the edge of each slice. Hold slice at each side of cut and twist in opposite directions.

COOK'S TIP
If using an electric table-top mixer there is no need to beat over hot water. If beating over hot water, check that the bottom of the bowl does not touch the water, or the eggs will set.

●310 calories/1295 kj per slice

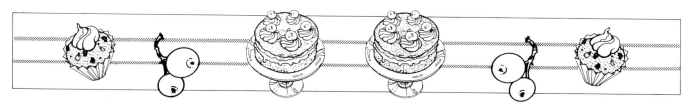

Cider cake

MAKES 6-8 SLICES

300 g/10 oz self-raising flour
2 teaspoons ground cinnamon
175 g/6 oz light soft brown sugar
175 g/6 oz seedless raisins
125 ml/4 fl oz vegetable oil
2 eggs, lightly beaten
175 ml/6 fl oz cider
vegetable oil, for greasing

TOPPING
1-2 cooking apples, peeled, cored, halved and sliced
lemon curd, to glaze

1 Heat the oven to 180C/350F/Gas 4. Lightly grease a deep, loose-based 20 cm/8 inch round cake tin. Line the sides and base with greaseproof paper, then lightly grease the paper with vegetable oil.

2 Sift the flour and cinnamon into a large bowl. Add the sugar, raisins, oil, eggs and cider and beat together with a wooden spoon until evenly blended.

3 Pour the mixture into the prepared tin. Arrange the apple slices over the top. Bake in the oven for about 1½ hours, until a fine, warmed skewer inserted into the

centre comes out clean. Cover with greaseproof paper during baking if the apples show signs of overbrowning.

4 Cool the cake for 5 minutes, then remove from the tin and peel off the lining paper. Place the right way up on a wire rack. Brush the apples with lemon curd, then leave the cake to cool completely.

Cook's Notes

 TIME
35 minutes preparation, 1½ hours baking, plus cooling time.

 STORAGE
The cake will stay moist for 4-5 days if kept in an airtight container.

 FREEZING
Cool cake completely, then wrap in foil, seal, label and freeze for up to 6 months. To serve: unwrap and defrost at room temperature for 4 hours, then glaze.

ECONOMY
Sweet, medium and dry cider are all suitable. To save opening a large bottle specially, buy a 440 ml/15½ fl oz can strong dry cider.

● 555 calories/2330 kj per portion

Zebra roll

MAKES 8 SLICES

50 g/2 oz plain flour
25 g/1 oz cocoa powder
pinch of baking powder (see Cook's tip)
3 large eggs
100 g/4 oz caster sugar
1 tablespoon hot water
extra caster sugar
vegetable oil, for greasing

FILLING

300 ml/½ pint whipping cream
2 tablespoons orange-flavoured liqueur (optional)
8 fancy chocolates, to decorate

1 Heat the oven to 200C/400F/Gas 6. Grease a 30 × 20 cm/ 12 × 8 inch Swiss roll tin, line with greaseproof paper, then grease the paper.
2 Sift flour, cocoa and baking powder.
3 Put eggs and sugar into a large heatproof bowl. Set over a pan of gently simmering water, making sure bottom of the bowl does not touch water. Using a rotary or hand-held electric whisk, beat until mixture is mousse-like and thick enough to hold trail of whisk for 3 seconds when beaters are lifted.
4 Remove bowl from the pan and whisk for a few minutes more, then fold in flour and water. Pour into prepared tin and spread evenly by gently tilting tin. Bake [!] for 12-14 minutes, until well risen.
5 Meanwhile, lay a sheet of greaseproof paper on top of a clean, damp tea-towel. Sprinkle paper thickly with caster sugar.
6 Turn baked cake out on to the sugared paper. Peel lining paper off then trim crusty edges with a sharp knife. Make a shallow cut along 1 short end, about 1 cm/½ inch from the edge. Roll up the cake with paper inside. Place seam-side down on a wire rack and leave to cool for 30 minutes.
7 Make the filling: whip cream, with the liqueur if using, until standing in soft peaks. Put one-quarter of cream into a piping bag with large star nozzle and reserve. Whip remaining cream until stiff.
8 Unroll cake, remove the paper and spread with stiffly whipped cream, then roll up again. Decorate with piped cream and chocolates. Serve on day of making.

Cook's Notes

TIME
Total preparation time is about 1¼ hours.

COOK'S TIP
Baking powder helps the cake to rise evenly.

WATCHPOINT
Bake without delay, otherwise the whisked mixture will lose volume.

FREEZING
Open freeze until solid, then pack in a rigid container, seal, label and return to freezer for up to 1 month. To serve: unwrap and defrost at room temperature for 3-4 hours then decorate the top with fancy chocolates.

●265 calories/1125 kj per slice.

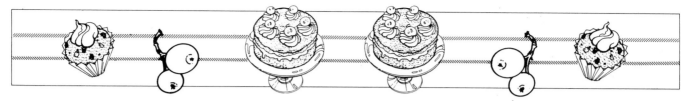

Iced applecake

MAKES 6-8 SLICES
225 g/8 oz plain flour
2 teaspoons baking powder
½ teaspoon salt
75 g/3 oz margarine or butter, diced
100 g/4 oz caster sugar
50 g/2 oz currants
1 egg, lightly beaten
100 ml/3½ fl oz milk
vegetable oil, for greasing

TO FINISH
2 dessert apples
25 g/1 oz butter, melted
50 g/2 oz caster sugar
¼ teaspoon ground cloves
50 g/2 oz icing sugar, sifted
2-3 teaspoons lemon juice or water

1 Heat the oven to 200C/400F/Gas 6. Generously grease a loose-based, deep 20 cm/8 inch round cake tin.
2 Sift the flour, baking powder and salt into a bowl. Add the margarine and rub it in with your fingertips, then stir in the sugar and currants. Make a well in the centre.
3 Pour in the egg and milk and stir with a fork until evenly mixed. Turn the mixture into the prepared tin and level the surface.
4 Peel, quarter and core then thinly slice the apples (see Cook's tip). Arrange the slices, overlapping, in circles on top of cake mixture. Brush the apples with melted butter, then sprinkle with the sugar and cloves.
5 Bake the cake in the oven for about 50 minutes, until firm to the touch at the centre. Cool the cake for 5 minutes, then remove from the tin and place on a wire rack with a plate or tray underneath.
6 Blend the icing sugar with just enough lemon juice to give a smooth, thick icing. Using a metal spoon, drizzle the icing over the top of the cake, allowing it to run down the sides. Leave the icing to set before cutting the cake into 6-8 wedges (see Serving ideas).

Cook's Notes

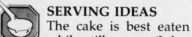

TIME
25 minutes preparation, plus 50 minutes baking. Allow a few minutes more for icing, plus setting time.

COOK'S TIP
Try to make the slices as even as possible and arrange them neatly, otherwise the finished cake will not look quite so attractive.

SERVING IDEAS
The cake is best eaten while still warm. (It becomes less light and more crumbly as it cools.)
The cake can also be served hot from the oven as a pudding, accompanied by custard or cream. In which case, omit the icing sugar and lemon juice.

● 450 calories/1900 kj per slice

Lemon and honey roll

MAKES 8-10 SLICES
75 g/3 oz plain flour
pinch of salt
3 large eggs
75 g/3 oz caster sugar
grated zest of 1 lemon
extra caster sugar
vegetable oil, for greasing

FILLING
175 g/6 oz full-fat soft cheese
4 teaspoons clear honey
icing sugar, for dredging

1 Heat the oven to 200C/400F/Gas 6. Grease a 33 × 23 cm/13 × 9 inch Swiss roll tin; line the tin with greaseproof paper and grease the lining paper.
2 Sift the flour with the salt.

3 Put the eggs, sugar and lemon zest in a large heatproof bowl. Set the bowl over a pan half full of gently simmering water. ⚠ Using a rotary or hand-held electric whisk, beat the mixture together until thick and foamy. Continue beating until the mixture is thick enough to hold the trail of the whisk for 3 seconds when the beaters are lifted.
4 Remove the bowl from the pan, whisk for a few minutes more until the mixture is cool, then lightly but thoroughly fold in the sifted flour, one-third at a time, using a large metal spoon.
5 Pour the mixture into the prepared tin and spread it evenly by gently tilting the tin. Bake the cake immediately in the oven for 8-10 minutes until the surface is golden and springs back when lightly pressed in the centre.
6 While the cake is baking, lay a sheet of greaseproof paper on top of a clean, damp tea-towel. Sprinkle the paper generously and evenly with caster sugar.
7 Turn the baked cake out on to the sugared paper. Trim off the crisp edges with a sharp knife. Make a shallow cut along 1 short end, about 1 cm/½ inch from the edge (see Cook's tip), then tightly roll up the cake with the paper inside. Place seam-side down on a wire rack and then leave to cool for about 30 minutes. ⚠ ✳
8 To make the filling: beat the cheese with the honey until soft and smoothly blended. Unroll the cake and remove the paper. Spread the cake with the filling, then gently roll it up again. Sift icing sugar thickly over the top. Serve the cake the day it is made.

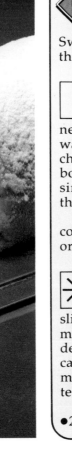

Cook's Notes

TIME
Preparation takes 10-15 minutes, depending on the type of whisk used; baking takes 8-10 minutes. Allow another 20-30 minutes for the cake to cool, and about 10 minutes for filling it.

COOK'S TIP
The shallow cut along the short end of the Swiss roll makes it easier to roll the cake without cracking.

WATCHPOINTS
If you use an electric table mixer, there is no need to place the bowl over hot water. If using a rotary whisk check that the bottom of the bowl does not touch the gently simmering water. If overheated, the eggs will begin to coagulate.
Do not leave the baked cake to cool longer than 20-30 minutes, or it may break when rolled.

FREEZING
This type of cake is best frozen while still slightly warm—it will then stay much fresher and moister once defrosted. Wrap the unfilled cake and freeze for up to 10 months. Defrost at room temperature for about 1 hour.

●225 calories/950 kj per slice

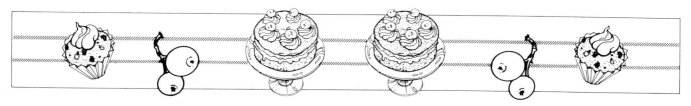

Banana and Brazil cake

MAKES 10 SLICES
75 g/3 oz soft tub margarine
100 g/4 oz light soft brown sugar
1 egg, lightly beaten
2 small bananas, mashed
100 g/4 oz plain flour
1 teaspoon baking powder
vegetable oil, for greasing

ICING
1 tablespoon clear honey
75 g/3 oz icing sugar, sifted
1-2 teaspoons cold water
25 g/1 oz shelled Brazil nuts,
    coarsely chopped

1 Heat the oven to 170C/325F/Gas 3. Lightly grease an 850 ml/1½ pint (500 g/1 lb) loaf tin; line the base with greaseproof paper, then grease the paper.

2 Put the margarine, sugar, egg and mashed bananas into a large bowl. Sift in the flour and baking powder, then beat with a wooden spoon for 1-2 minutes until evenly blended.
3 Turn the mixture into the prepared tin and level the surface. Bake in the oven for 1-1¼ hours, until browned and firm to the touch (see Cook's tips).
4 Cool the cake for 10 minutes, then turn out of the tin and carefully peel off the lining paper. Place the right way up on a wire rack and leave to cool completely.
5 Make the icing: mix the honey into the icing sugar with a large metal spoon, then stir in just enough water to give a thick pouring consistency (see Cook's tips).
6 Place a plate under the wire rack. Spoon the icing over the top of the cake, allowing it to run down the sides. Leave for 10 minutes to firm slightly, then sprinkle with the nuts. Leave to set before cutting.

Cook's Notes

 TIME
20 minutes preparation, plus 1-1¼ hours baking. Allow extra time for cooling, icing and setting.

COOK'S TIPS
To test that the cake is cooked, insert a warmed fine skewer into the centre: it should come out free of any sticky uncooked mixture.
    Add the water a few drops at a time and mix well. If you do make the icing too thin, sift in a little extra icing sugar. The icing becomes transparent when set.

 STORAGE
The uniced cake will keep for up to 6 days in an airtight container.

● 190 calories/800 kj per slice

Peach coffeecake

MAKES 6 SQUARES

425 g/15 oz can peach slices, drained
225 g/8 oz plain flour
2 teaspoons baking powder
½ teaspoon salt
75 g/3 oz margarine or butter, diced
100 g/4 oz caster sugar
1 egg, beaten
100 ml/3½ fl oz milk
vegetable oil, for greasing

TO FINISH
25 g/1 oz butter, melted
50 g/2 oz light soft brown sugar
½ teaspoon ground cinnamon
50 g/2 oz icing sugar, sifted
about 1 tablespoon water

1 Heat the oven to 200C/400F/Gas 6. Grease a deep 18 cm/7 inch square cake tin with a loose base.
2 Pat the peaches dry on absorbent paper, then cut any thick slices lengthways in half. Set aside.
3 Sift the flour, baking powder and salt into a bowl. Add the margarine and rub it in with your fingertips, then stir in the sugar. Add the egg and milk and stir until evenly mixed. Turn the mixture into the prepared tin and level the surface.
4 Arrange the peach slices in neat rows over the top (see Cook's tip). Brush with melted butter, then sprinkle with brown sugar and cinnamon.
5 Bake in the oven for about 50 minutes, until firm to the touch at the centre. Cool the cake for 5 minutes, then remove from the tin and place on a wire rack.
6 Blend the icing sugar with enough water to give the consistency of unwhipped double cream. Trickle the icing over the peaches (see Preparation) and leave to set.
7 Serve the cake while still warm, cut into squares (see Serving ideas).

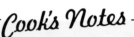

Cook's Notes

TIME
Preparation (including icing) takes 20-25 minutes. Baking time is 50 minutes.

SERVING IDEAS
This American-style cake is usually served warm with morning coffee— hence its name; it is just as nice with tea.

COOK'S TIP
Make sure you arrange the peaches neatly. They will make the finished cake even more attractive.

PREPARATION
How to ice the peach coffeecake:

Using a zig-zag or squiggly action, pour the icing in a stream from a spoon over the top of the cake. This is called 'drizzling' or trickling.

●490 calories/2050 kj per square

Cranberry coconut cake

MAKES 8 SLICES

175 g/6 oz cranberry sauce (see Buying guide)

225 g/8 oz self-raising flour
1 teaspoon bicarbonate of soda
½ teaspoon salt
1 teaspoon ground cinnamon
225 g/8 oz soft brown sugar
50 g/2 oz desiccated coconut
75 g/3 oz grated carrot
2 eggs, beaten
150 ml/¼ pint vegetable oil
vegetable oil, for greasing

TOPPING
1 tablespoon apricot jam
2 tablespoons desiccated or long strand coconut, toasted if liked

1 Heat the oven to 180C/350F/Gas 4. Grease a deep 18 cm/7 inch round cake tin. Line the base with grease-proof paper and grease the paper.
2 Sift the flour into a bowl with the bicarbonate of soda, salt and cinnamon. Add the cranberry sauce, sugar, coconut, carrot, eggs and oil, then beat with a wooden spoon for about 2 minutes, until well blended.
3 Turn the mixture into the prepared tin. Bake in the oven for about 65 minutes, or until the cake feels firm to the touch when pressed.
4 Cool the cake for 5 minutes, then remove from the tin and peel off the lining paper. Leave the cake, the right way up, on a wire rack to cool completely.✳
5 Transfer the cake to a serving plate. Spread the top with the jam, then sprinkle over the coconut.

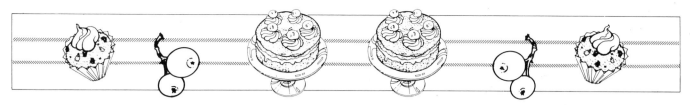

Orange yoghurt cake

MAKES 8-10 SLICES

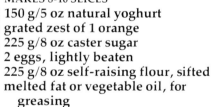

150 g/5 oz natural yoghurt
grated zest of 1 orange
225 g/8 oz caster sugar
2 eggs, lightly beaten
225 g/8 oz self-raising flour, sifted
melted fat or vegetable oil, for
    greasing

TO DECORATE
thinly pared rind of ½ orange
100 g/4 oz icing sugar, sifted
2-3 teaspoons warm water

1 Heat the oven to 180C/350F/Gas 4. Grease a 1.25-1.5 L/2-2½ pint loaf tin. Line the base of the tin with greaseproof paper, then grease the paper.
2 Put the yoghurt into a bowl, then stir in the orange zest and caster sugar. Using a wooden spoon, beat in the eggs a little at a time, then beat in the flour. (The mixture will be runny.)
3 Pour the mixture into the prepared tin. Bake in the oven for 45-50 minutes, until a warmed fine skewer inserted into the centre comes out clean.
4 Cool the cake for 5 minutes, then turn out of the tin and peel off the lining paper. Turn the cake the right way up, then leave on a wire rack to cool completely.
5 Meanwhile, cut the orange rind into matchstick-sized strips. Drop the strips into boiling water and simmer for 1 minute. Drain, then rinse under cold running water and dry thoroughly on absorbent paper.
6 When the cake is cold, make the icing: blend the icing sugar with enough warm water to give a stiff coating consistency. Using a palette knife, spread the icing over the top of the cake (see Cook's tip). Leave the icing to set, then decorate with the strips of orange rind.

Cook's Notes

 TIME
10-15 minutes preparation, plus 45-50 minutes baking. Allow 1½ hours for cooling, icing and decorating.

 STORAGE
The un-iced cake will keep for up to 1 week in an airtight container. The iced cake is best served within 48 hours, as the icing dries out.

COOK'S TIP
Dip the knife in hot water as you work; this gives a smooth, shiny finish.

 WATCHPOINT
Do not add the strips of orange until the icing is set, or the colour will run and spoil the look of the cake.

●295 calories/1225 kj per slice

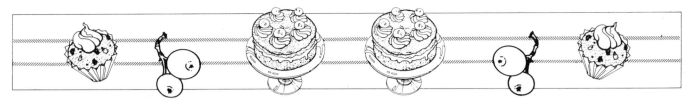

Chocolate rum cake

MAKES 6-8 SLICES

100 g/4 oz self-raising flour
½ teaspoon bicarbonate of soda
40 g/1½ oz cocoa powder
100 ml/3½ fl oz cold water
2 tablespoons dark rum
100 g/4 oz margarine or butter,
    softened
225 g/8 oz caster sugar
2 eggs, beaten
50 g/2 oz ground almonds
melted fat or vegetable oil, for
    greasing

1 Heat the oven to 170C/325F/Gas 3. Grease a deep 18 cm/7 inch round tin with a loose base. Line the base of the tin with greaseproof paper, then grease the paper.

2 Sift the flour with the bicarbonate of soda. Put the cocoa powder into a small bowl and gradually blend in the water and rum.

3 Beat the margarine and caster sugar together until pale and fluffy. Add the eggs, a little at a time, beating vigorously after each addition. Using a large metal spoon, stir in the cocoa mixture, ground almonds and sifted flour, in alternate spoonfuls.

4 Turn the mixture into the prepared tin and level the surface. Bake in the oven for about 65 minutes, until the cake is springy to the touch at the centre.

5 Cool the cake for 10 minutes, then run a palette knife around the sides and remove from the tin. Carefully peel off the lining paper. Leave the cake on a wire rack to cool completely. Wrap and store for 24 hours before cutting to allow the texture to become soft and moist.

Peach layer cake

MAKES 6 SLICES

3 eggs, separated
100 g/4 oz caster sugar
grated zest of ½ lemon
1 tablespoon lemon juice
50 g/2 oz fine semolina
15 g/½ oz ground almonds
icing sugar, for dusting
vegetable oil, for greasing

FILLING

150 ml/¼ pint whipping cream
400 g/14 oz can peach slices, well
    drained

1 Heat the oven to 180C/350F/Gas 4. Grease a deep 20 cm/8 inch sandwich tin. Line the base with greaseproof paper, then grease the paper.

2 In a large bowl, beat the egg yolks, caster sugar and lemon zest with a wooden spoon until thick and pale. Beat in the lemon juice, a little at a time. Stir in the semolina and almonds, then leave to stand for 10 minutes (see Cook's tips).

3 In a clean, dry bowl, whisk the egg whites until standing in soft peaks. Using a large metal spoon, fold the egg whites into the semolina mixture (see Cook's tips).

4 Spoon the mixture into the prepared tin and bake in the oven for 30-40 minutes, until risen and golden and firm to the touch. Cool for 10 minutes, then turn out of the tin on to a wire rack. Peel off the lining paper and leave to cool.

5 To serve: cut the cake in half horizontally with a long, serrated knife. Whip the cream until standing in soft peaks. Place 1 cake layer on a serving plate and spread with half the cream. Arrange the peaches over the cream, then spread over the rest of the cream. Place the remaining cake, cut side down, on top (see Cook's tips). Sift a little icing sugar over the top of the cake.

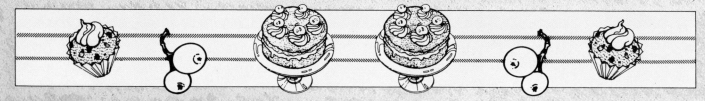

Battenburg cake

MAKES 6 SLICES
100 g/4 oz butter or margarine, softened
100 g/4 oz caster sugar
2 eggs, lightly beaten
1 teaspoon vanilla flavouring
100 g/4 oz self-raising flour, sifted
few drops of red food colouring
vegetable oil, for greasing

TO FINISH
5 tablespoons apricot jam
225 g/8 oz almond marzipan
caster sugar, for dredging

1 Heat the oven to 190C/375F/Gas 5. Grease a deep 18 cm/7 inch square tin with a loose base, line the base with greaseproof paper, then grease the paper.
2 Cut a rectangle of foil, measuring 40 × 30 cm/16 × 12 inches. Fold across in half, then across again in quarters to make a strip of 4 thicknesses, 30 × 10 cm/12 × 4 inches.
3 Place the foil strip across the centre of the tin (to divide it in half) and fold both ends flush with the sides of the tin. Secure the ends in place with paper clips, then grease the foil.
4 Beat the butter and caster sugar until pale and fluffy. Add the eggs, a little at a time, beating thoroughly after each addition (see Cook's tips), then beat in the vanilla. Using a large metal spoon, fold in the flour.
5 Turn half the mixture into one-half of the prepared tin and level the surface. Tint the remaining mixture pink with food colouring, then turn into the other half and level surface.
6 Bake just above the centre of the oven for about 30 minutes, until the cakes are golden and springy to the touch (see Cook's tips). Leave in the tin to cool (see Cook's tips).
7 Remove the paper clips. Remove the cake from the tin. Slide a palette knife underneath each cake to loosen it from the lining paper, then carefully separate the cakes by easing them away from the foil.
8 Using a sharp serrated knife, trim the cakes so that they are exactly the same size. [!] Cut each cake in half lengthways to make 4 strips.
9 Sieve the jam into a small saucepan and stir over low heat until melted. Use some of the jam to stick the cakes together in a chequerboard pattern (see Steps 1 and 2).
10 Knead the marzipan until smooth. [!] Sprinkle the work surface generously with caster sugar, then roll out the marzipan to a rectangle 28 × 16 cm/11 × 6½ inches (see Cook's tips). Trim the edges with a sharp knife.
11 Brush the top of the cake with jam, then cover in the marzipan (see Steps 3 and 4).
12 Place the cake, seam side down, on a serving plate. Crimp each long top edge of marzipan to decorate, then use a knife to mark a diamond pattern on the top of the cake. Sprinkle caster sugar over.

TIME
Total preparation time (including baking, cooling and finishing) is 1½ hours.

COOK'S TIPS
If the mixture shows signs of curdling, add 1 teaspoon of the flour with the next addition of egg.

If the cakes have domed slightly, press them gently with a clean tea-towel while still hot to give a flat surface.

Because these cakes are very fragile, they are left in the tin to cool and firm up.

If the marzipan sticks during rolling out, run a palette knife underneath to loosen it.

! WATCHPOINTS
It is essential to make the cakes precisely the same size, otherwise the cake will be misshapen.

Do not attempt to roll out the marzipan if it is cold and stiff as it will crack badly.

● 485 calories/2025 kj per slice

ASSEMBLING THE CAKE

1 *Place 1 pink and 1 plain strip side by side. Brush the adjacent sides with jam, then press the cakes together. Brush top with jam.*

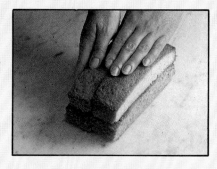

2 *Use remaining strips to make second layer, arranging them in a chequerboard pattern and sticking them together with jam.*

3 *Place the cake, jam side down, across 1 short end of the marzipan, then brush the remaining 3 sides of the cake with jam.*

4 *Carefully roll the cake up in the marzipan, then press the join firmly to seal. Trim both ends of the cake to neaten.*

Fudgy coffee cake

MAKES 8 SLICES

175 g/6 oz self-raising flour
1½ teaspoons baking powder
175 g/6 oz soft tub margarine
175 g/6 oz light soft brown sugar
3 eggs
1 tablespoon coffee and chicory
   essence
2-3 tablespoons apricot jam, for
   filling
vegetable oil, for greasing

FUDGY ICING

1 tablespoon coffee and chicory
   essence
2-3 tablespoons milk
40 g/1½ oz soft tub margarine
few drops of vanilla flavouring
275 g/10 oz icing sugar, sifted

1 Heat the oven to 170C/325F/Gas 3. Grease two 3.5 cm/1½ inch deep, 19 cm/7½ inch round sandwich tins. Line each base with grease-proof paper, then grease the paper.

2 Sift flour and baking powder into a large bowl. Add margarine, brown sugar, eggs and essence and beat with a wooden spoon for 1-2 minutes until evenly blended. Divide mixture equally between prepared tins and level each surface. Bake in the oven for 35-40 minutes, until springy to the touch.

3 Cool cakes for 5 minutes, then turn out of tins and peel off lining papers. Leave cakes on a wire rack to cool completely.

4 Sandwich cold cakes together with jam, then place on a wire rack with a plate underneath.

5 Make the icing: put the essence, 2 tablespoons milk, margarine and vanilla into a small, heavy-based pan. Stir over low heat until the margarine has melted, then bring to the boil. Pour immediately on to the sifted icing sugar and beat with a wooden spoon until blended. If very stiff, beat in remaining milk.

6 Quickly spread the icing over the top and sides of the cake. ⚠ Mark into wedges while the icing is still soft, then leave for about 30 minutes to set. ⚠ The cake is best served on the day it is iced.

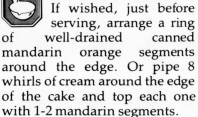

Rose marble cake

MAKES 12 SLICES

225 g/8 oz self-raising flour
2 teaspoons baking powder
225 g/8 oz soft tub margarine
225 g/8 oz caster sugar
4 eggs
2 tablespoons rose water (see
  Buying guide)
few drops of red food
  colouring
½ teaspoon vanilla essence
melted fat or vegetable oil, for
  greasing

ICING
100 g/4 oz icing sugar, sifted
1 tablespoon rose water
1-2 tablespoons water
crystallized rose petals, to decorate
  (see Buying guide)

1 Heat the oven to 180C/350F/Gas 4. Generously grease a 1.5 L/2½ pint plain ring mould. [!]

2 Sift the flour and baking powder into a large bowl. Add the soft margarine, sugar and eggs and mix well with a wooden spoon, then beat for about 2 minutes, until well blended.

3 Turn half the mixture into a separate bowl. Stir the rose water into one half and tint pink with a few drops of food colouring. Stir the vanilla essence into the other half.

4 Place alternate spoonfuls of the 2 mixtures in the mould. Draw the blade of a knife through the mixture, first one way and then the other. [!] Level the surface of the mixture carefully, taking care not to mix the colours too much. Bake in the oven for about 45 minutes, until a fine warmed skewer inserted in the centre comes out clean.

5 Let the cake stand in the tin for 3 minutes, then turn it out on a wire rack. Leave to cool completely. [✳]

6 Make the icing: blend the icing sugar with the rose water and gradually add enough water to give a smooth, runny consistency. Spoon the icing over the top and let it trickle down the sides. Scatter a few crystallized rose petals over the top and leave to set. Transfer to a serving plate.

TIME
The cake takes about 1 hour to make and bake. Allow about 1 hour for cooling, and 5-10 minutes for icing, plus setting time.

BUYING GUIDE
You can buy rose water from most chemists, and crystallized rose petals from delicatessens.

WATCHPOINT
Take care to grease the mould well so that the baked cake will turn out of the tin easily, without breaking.

Resist the temptation to 'over-swirl' the mixture before baking as this will make the marbling less noticeable. Draw the knife through the mixture once only in each direction.

FREEZING
Enclose the cold cake in a polythene bag, seal, label and freeze for up to 3 months. To serve: defrost the cake in its wrappings for 2-3 hours at room temperature, then unwrap and place on a wire rack. Ice and decorate as shown in the method.

STORAGE
This cake will keep for up to 2 weeks in an air-tight tin.

●340 calories/1425 kj per slice

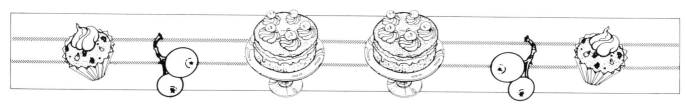

Madeira cake

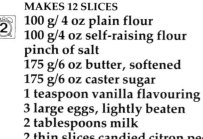

MAKES 12 SLICES
100 g/ 4 oz plain flour
100 g/4 oz self-raising flour
pinch of salt
175 g/6 oz butter, softened
175 g/6 oz caster sugar
1 teaspoon vanilla flavouring
3 large eggs, lightly beaten
2 tablespoons milk
2 thin slices candied citron peel
(see Buying guide)
vegetable oil, for greasing

1 Heat the oven to 170C/325F/Gas 3. Grease a deep 18 cm/7 inch round cake tin, line the sides and base with greaseproof paper, then lightly grease the paper.
2 Sift the flours with the salt.
3 In a separate bowl, beat butter and sugar until very pale and fluffy, then beat in vanilla. Add the eggs, a little at a time, beating thoroughly

until blended after each addition.
4 Using a large metal spoon, fold in the sifted flours, then stir in milk. Turn the mixture into the prepared tin and level the surface.
5 Bake the cake in the oven for 1 hour, then gently arrange the citron peel on the top. (The top may have cracked slightly.) Return to the

oven for a further 15 minutes, or until firm to the touch and a warmed fine skewer inserted into the centre comes out clean.
6 Cool the cake for 10-15 minutes, then turn out of the tin and peel off the lining paper. Place the cake the right way up on a wire rack and leave to cool completely.

Cook's Notes

TIME
15 minutes preparation and 1¼ hours baking. Allow 2-3 hours for the cake to cool completely.

DID YOU KNOW
This English cake was very popular during the 19th century and was traditionally served with a glass of Madeira wine — hence its name. Homemade Madeira cake is lighter, and has a much more 'spongy' and crumbly texture than commercial varieties.

STORAGE
Madeira cake will keep for 2-3 weeks in an airtight container in a cool place.

BUYING GUIDE
Candied citron peel can be difficult to obtain: try specialist delicatessens and high-class food stores. The peel is sold by the piece — slice off the amount you need, wrap remainder in cling film and keep in a cool place.

●250 calories/1025 kj per slice

Rich cherry cake

MAKES 6-8 SLICES

225 g/8 oz glacé cherries, halved
   (see Preparation)
75 g/3 oz plain flour
175 g/6 oz butter, softened
175 g/6 oz caster sugar
3 eggs, beaten
50 g/2 oz ground almonds
75 g/3 oz self-raising flour
2 tablespoons milk
vegetable oil, for greasing

1 Heat the oven to 180C/350F/Gas 4. Grease a deep 18 cm/7 inch round cake tin, line the sides and base with greaseproof paper, then grease the paper.

2 Put the cherries into a bowl. Sift over 1 tablespoon plain flour, then turn the cherries until lightly coated. Reserve.

3 Beat the butter with the sugar until very light and fluffy. Add the eggs, a little at a time, beating

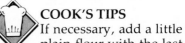

TIME
Preparation (including baking) takes about 1¾-2 hours.

STORAGE
The cake will keep fresh and moist for up to 3 weeks in an airtight container.

PREPARATION
To prevent the cherries sinking, their sticky coating must be removed: place the halved cherries in a sieve and rinse under hot running water; shake well, then spread out on absorbent paper and leave to dry completely.

COOK'S TIPS
If necessary, add a little plain flour with the last addition of egg to prevent the mixture curdling.
  Try to avoid banging the tin once the mixture has been added and do not slam the oven door as this may cause the cherries to sink a little.

● 585 calories/2455 kj per slice

thoroughly after each addition (see Cook's tips). Stir in the ground almonds.

4 Sift in the flours and fold in with a large metal spoon. Fold in the milk, then lightly fold in the reserved cherries. Turn the mixture into the prepared tin, making sure that the cherries are not grouped together. Level the surface, then make a shallow hollow in the centre.

5 Bake in the oven (see Cook's tips) for about 1¼ hours, or until a warmed fine skewer inserted into the centre comes out clean. Cool the cake for 5 minutes, then turn out of the tin on to a wire rack and carefully peel off the lining paper. Turn the cake the right way up, then leave to cool completely.

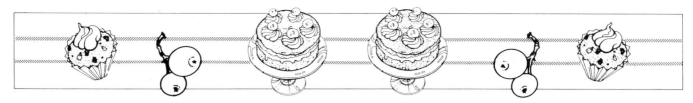

Yummy chocolate cake

MAKES 8-10 SLICES

200 g/7 oz self-raising flour
2 tablespoons cocoa powder
pinch of salt
225 g/8 oz caster sugar
2 large eggs
5 tablespoons evaporated milk
5 tablespoons water
1 teaspoon vanilla flavouring
100 g/4 oz margarine, melted
vegetable oil, for greasing

FILLING AND TOPPING

225 g/8 oz icing sugar
40 g/1½ oz powdered drinking
 chocolate
65 g/2½ oz margarine, melted
3 tablespoons hot milk
1 teaspoon vanilla flavouring

1 Heat the oven to 180C/350F/Gas 4. Grease two 20 cm/8 inch sandwich tins, line each base with greaseproof paper, then grease the paper.

2 Sift the flour, cocoa and salt into a large bowl. Stir in the sugar, then make a well in the centre. Beat the eggs with the milk, water and vanilla, then add to the dry ingredients together with the margarine and beat until blended.

3 Divide the mixture equally between the 2 prepared tins. Burst any large air bubbles with the point of a knife, then bake the cakes in the oven for 20-25 minutes, or until springy to the touch.

4 Cool the cakes for a few minutes, then turn out of the tins and peel off the lining papers. Leave the cakes, the right way up, on a wire rack to cool completely.

5 Make the filling and topping: sift the icing sugar and drinking chocolate into a bowl, then beat in the margarine, milk and vanilla. Leave for 15-30 minutes, until it begins to thicken.

6 Place 1 cake on a serving plate and spread with half the chocolate mixture. Place the other cake on top and spread with the remaining chocolate mixture. Leave for about 30 minutes, to firm, before cutting.

Cook's Notes

TIME
35-40 minutes preparation (including baking), plus cooling time for the cakes. Allow extra time for the filling and topping.

STORAGE
The finished cake will keep for about 4 days in an airtight container.

FOR CHILDREN
Decorate the top of the cake with sugar-coated chocolate buttons, sugar flowers or coloured sugar strands just before serving.

●510 calories/2150 kj per slice

Crystallized fruit cake

MAKES 10 SLICES

175 g/6 oz butter or margarine
175 g/6 oz caster sugar
225 g/8 oz plain flour
3 eggs
½ teaspoon ground mixed spice
½ teaspoon ground cinnamon
100 g/4 oz sultanas
100 g/4 oz seedless raisins
100 g/4 oz currants
100 g/4 oz glacé cherries, quartered
1 tablespoon milk

TO DECORATE AND GLAZE

40 g/1½ oz crystallized pineapple,
   cut into small chunks
40 g/1½ oz glacé cherries, halved
25 g/1 oz split almonds
3 tablespoons apricot jam
1 tablespoon water
½ teaspoon lemon juice

1 Heat the oven to 170C/325F/Gas 3. Grease and line a deep 15 cm/6 inch square cake tin (see Preparation).
2 In a large bowl, beat butter and sugar together with a hand-held electric whisk until pale and fluffy. Beat in the eggs 1 at a time (see Cook's tip) until evenly incorporated.
3 Sift flour and spices into a bowl. Fold flour and fruit alternately into egg mixture. Fold in the milk. Turn the mixture into the prepared tin and level the surface. Arrange pineapple, glacé cherries and almonds over the top of the cake.
4 Stand the tin on several layers of brown paper on a baking tray. Bake in the oven for 1 hour, then lower the temperature to 150C/300F/Gas 2 and bake for a further 1½-2 hours.
5 Cool cake for 5 minutes, then turn out of the tin on to a wire rack and peel off paper. Turn the right way up, then cool completely.
6 Make glaze: put jam and water in a pan and boil for 2 minutes. Stir in lemon juice, then sieve, return to pan and heat gently. Brush over fruit on top of cake. Leave the glaze to cool and set before serving.

Cook's Notes

TIME
Preparation takes about 45 minutes and cooking about 2½-3 hours. Allow an extra 20 minutes for finishing.

PREPARATION
Line the sides of the tin with a double thickness of greaseproof which comes 4 cm/1½ inches above the top of the tin. Line the base with a double thickness of greaseproof. Lightly grease the paper. Wrap a band of brown paper around the outside of the tin and secure in place with fine string.

COOK'S TIP
Add 1 tablespoon flour with each egg after the first to prevent curdling.

FREEZING
Wrap in a polythene bag, then seal, label and freeze for up to 6 months. To serve: defrost the cake at room temperature for 4-5 hours then glaze before serving.

STORAGE
Keeps in an airtight container for 2 weeks.

●445 calories/1875 kj per slice

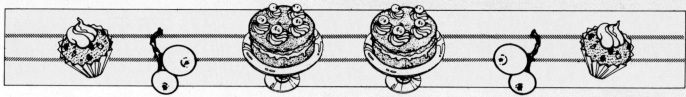

Victoria sandwich cake

MAKES 8-10 SLICES
225 g/8 oz self-raising flour
pinch of salt
225 g/8 oz butter softened
  (see Economy)
225 g/8 oz caster sugar
4 large eggs, lightly beaten
melted fat or vegetable oil,
  for greasing

FILLING
3-4 tablespoons red jam
150 ml/¼ pint whipping cream
  (optional)
caster or icing sugar for dredging

1 Heat the oven to 180C/350F/Gas 4. Grease two 4 cm/1½ inch deep, 19 cm/7½ inch sandwich tins. Line the base of each tin with greaseproof paper, then grease the paper.
2 Sift the flour with the salt and set aside. Using a wooden spoon, or a hand-held electric whisk, beat the butter and caster sugar until pale and fluffy. ! Add the eggs a little at a time, beating thoroughly after each addition. ! When the eggs have all been incorporated, fold in sifted flour, about one-third at a time, using a large metal spoon. !
3 Divide the mixture equally between the prepared tins and level each surface. Bake in the oven for 40-45 minutes, ! until the cakes are well risen and springy to the touch at the centre.
4 Leave the cakes in the tins for 30 seconds, then turn out on to a wire rack and remove the lining paper. Turn the cakes the right way up and leave to cool completely. ✳
5 Spread 1 cake with jam. If filling with cream, whip until thick, then spread over the underside of the remaining cake. Sandwich the cakes together, then sift caster or icing sugar over the top.
6 Place the cake on a serving plate; serve immediately or keep in a cool place for up to 2 hours.

This classic English cake is a popular tea-time treat. The basic mixture is wonderfully versatile, and can be flavoured in many different ways.
  Lemon sandwich: beat in the grated zest of 1 lemon before adding eggs. Sandwich the cakes together with 3-4 tablespoons lemon curd. Spread the top with lemon curd. Decorate with lemon jelly slices.
  Chocolate sandwich: blend 1½ tablespoons cocoa powder with 2 tablespoons hot water; allow to cool slightly, then beat into the mixture before adding the eggs. Sandwich the cakes together with jam and a layer of lightly whipped cream. To finish the cake: sift a little icing sugar over the top of the cake, then decorate by piping a lattice of melted chocolate cake covering over the top. Plain dessert chocolate can also be used.

Orange sandwich: beat in the grated zest of 1 orange before adding the eggs. Sandwich the cakes with marmalade or cream. If liked, whip 150 ml/¼ pint of whipping cream until it will hold its shape; spread some of the cream over the top of the cake, then use the remainder to pipe rosettes around the edge. Top each rosette with a drained canned mandarin orange segment. Fresh orange segments can be used but canned mandarins are daintier and juicier.

Coffee and hazelnut sandwich: blend 2½ teaspoons instant coffee powder with 1 tablespoon boiling water; allow to cool slightly, then beat into the mixture before adding the eggs. Sandwich the cakes together with 3-4 tablespoons chocolate hazelnut spread. Cover the top with chocolate hazelnut spread and decorate with toasted skinned hazelnut kernels.

Coconut sandwich: add 2-3 drops vanilla flavouring when beating in the eggs. Sandwich the cakes together with 3-4 tablespoons red cherry jam. Blend 100 g/4 oz sifted icing sugar with 1 tablespoon warm water and use to ice the top of the cake. While the icing is still soft, scatter the top thickly with desiccated coconut; arrange sliced glacé cherries around the top edge.

Cook's Notes

TIME
Preparation takes 20-25 minutes (depending on the method of beating); baking takes 40-45 minutes and cooling at least 2 hours. Allow a few minutes more for filling and decorating.

WATCHPOINTS
The butter and sugar must be beaten thoroughly together, or cake will not have a light texture. Stop beating every so often and scrape down the sides of the bowl so that no sugar crystals are left undissolved.

If the eggs are used straight from the refrigerator, or added too quickly, the mixture may curdle. (It will look lumpy and grainy instead of smooth and creamy.) Curdling can be remedied by adding 1 tablespoon of the sifted flour with the next addition of egg, but the cake will have a slightly heavier texture.

Use a cutting, figure-of-eight action to incorporate the flour. Do not stir or beat at this stage or the cake will not rise well.

Resist opening the oven door until the end of the minimum recommended baking time. The sudden draught of cold air will cause the cakes to sink.

ECONOMY
For a shallower cake, reduce the ingredients by one quarter and bake for 25-30 minutes. Margarine can be used instead of butter.

STORAGE
The unfilled cakes will keep for up to 1 week in an airtight container.

FREEZING
Wrap the unfilled cakes individually, or together with waxed paper in between, and freeze for up to 1 year. Defrost in wrappings for about 4 hours at room temperature.

● 490 calories/2050 kj per slice

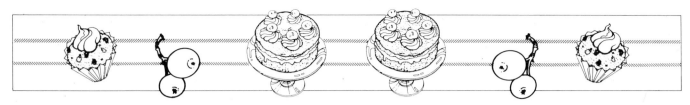

Orange marmalade cake

MAKES 8-10 SLICES
250 g/9 oz plain flour
1 teaspoon baking powder
½ teaspoon salt
½ teaspoon ground ginger
150 g/5 oz caster sugar
100 g/4 oz margarine, diced
200 g/7 oz coarse cut orange
marmalade
125 ml/4 fl oz milk
vegetable oil, for greasing

1 Heat the oven to 190C/375F/Gas 5. Lightly grease a loose-based 18 cm/ 7 inch square tin, line sides and base with greaseproof paper, then grease the paper.
2 Sift the flour with the baking powder, salt and ginger into a bowl. Stir in the sugar. Add the margarine and rub it in with your fingertips until the mixture resembles even-

sized breadcrumbs, then make a well in the centre of the mixture.
3 Add 50 g/2 oz marmalade and the milk and mix with a large metal spoon until thoroughly blended. Turn the mixture into the prepared tin and level the surface. Using a fork, gently spread the remaining marmalade over the top, to within 1 cm/½ inch of sides. (It will scorch if taken right to the edges.)
4 Bake the cake in the oven for

50-60 minutes, or until a warmed fine skewer inserted into the centre comes out with no uncooked cake mixture clinging to it. Cover the tin with greaseproof paper after 35 minutes baking to prevent the marmalade topping scorching.
5 Cool the cake for 5 minutes, then remove from the tin and carefully peel off the lining paper. Place the cake on a wire rack and leave to cool completely (see Storage).

Cook's Notes

 TIME
30 minutes preparation and 50-60 minutes baking, plus cooling time.

STORAGE
The cake is ready for cutting once it is cold. For a more mellow flavour, wrap in foil and then store in an airtight container for 2-3 days (and up to 5 days).

 VARIATIONS
Try other marmalades, such as tangerine or lime. Ginger preserve can be used, but in this case omit the ground ginger. Plain wholemeal flour can replace the white flour and other ground spices, such as cinnamon, can be used instead of ginger.

●355 calories/1475 kj per slice

60

Pineapple sponge

MAKES 6-8 SLICES
75 g/3 oz plain flour
1/2 teaspoon ground mixed spice
1/4 teaspoon ground ginger
3 large eggs
75 g/3 oz caster sugar
vegetable oil, for greasing

FILLING AND TOPPING
375 g/13 oz can crushed pineapple,
    drained with syrup reserved
25 g/1 oz custard powder
2 teaspoons lemon juice
150 ml/1/4 pint whipping cream

1 Heat the oven to 190C/375F/Gas 5. Lightly grease two 18 cm/7 inch sandwich tins, line the base of each with greaseproof paper, then lightly grease the paper.
2 Sift the flour with the spices.
3 Put the eggs and sugar into a large heatproof bowl. Set the bowl over a pan half-full of gently simmering water. Using a rotary or hand-held electric whisk, beat until the mixture will hold the trail of the whisk for 3 seconds when the beaters are lifted.
4 Remove the bowl from the pan and whisk for a few minutes more until the mixture is cool. Using a large metal spoon, fold in the sifted flour one-third at a time.
5 Divide the mixture equally between the prepared tins and spread evenly by gently tilting the tins. Bake immediately in the oven for 15 minutes until golden and springy to the touch.
6 Leave to stand for 2-3 seconds, then turn out on to a wire rack. Peel off the lining paper, turn the cakes right way up and leave until cold.
7 Meanwhile, make the filling: make up the reserved pineapple syrup to 300 ml/1/2 pint with water.
8 In a bowl, blend the custard powder with some of the pineapple liquid. In a pan, bring the remaining liquid to the boil, then stir into the custard. Return mixture to pan and simmer, stirring, for 1-2 minutes until thickened.
9 Remove from the heat and stir in the crushed pineapple and lemon juice. Leave to cool completely.
10 Assemble the cake: spread 1 sponge with two-thirds of the pineapple mixture. Place the remaining sponge on top and spread with the rest of the pineapple mixture, to within 1 cm/1/2 inch of the edges. Whip the cream until standing in soft peaks, then pipe around the edge (see Cook's tip). Serve as soon as possible.

Cook's Notes

 TIME
Total preparation time is about 1 1/2 hours.

 COOK'S TIP
Use a teaspoon to drop small rounds of cream on the cake instead of piping it.

●305 calories/1285 kj per slice

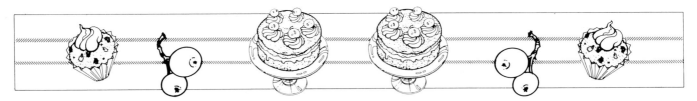

Carrot and almond cake

MAKES 6-8 SLICES

3 large eggs, separated
2 drops almond flavouring
grated zest of 1 orange
100 g/4 oz caster sugar
1 tablespoon orange-flavoured
　liqueur or orange juice
175 g/6 oz carrots, cooked, drained
　and puréed
100 g/4 oz ground almonds
50 g/2 oz ground rice
15 g/½ oz flaked almonds
icing sugar, for dusting
sweetened whipped cream or
　natural yoghurt, to serve
margarine or butter, for greasing

1 Heat the oven to 170C/325F/Gas 3. Generously grease a loose-based, deep 18 cm/7 inch round tin.
2 Put the egg yolks, almond flavouring and orange zest in a large bowl and whisk together with a hand-held electric whisk (see Cook's tips). Add the caster sugar, a little at a time, and continue whisking for a further 3-5 minutes, until the mixture is pale and mousse-like.
3 Whisk in the liqueur and carrot purée, then stir in the ground almonds and ground rice.
4 In a clean, dry bowl and using clean beaters, whisk the egg whites until standing in stiff peaks. Using a large metal spoon, stir one-third of the egg whites into the carrot and almond mixture, then fold in the remainder.
5 Turn the mixture into the prepared tin, level the surface and sprinkle the flaked almonds around the edge. Bake in the oven just above the centre, for 55-60 minutes, until a warmed fine skewer inserted in the centre comes out clean.
6 Cool the cake for 15 minutes, then remove from the tin (see Cook's tips) and leave on a wire rack to cool completely.
7 Sift a little icing sugar over the top of the cake and serve with a bowl of sweetened cream handed round separately.

Grape gâteau

MAKES 6-8 SLICES
75 g/3 oz plain flour
pinch of salt
pinch of baking powder
3 large eggs
150 g/5 oz caster sugar
vegetable oil, for greasing

FILLING AND DECORATION
300 ml/½ pint double or whipping
  cream
3 tablespoons kirsch
2 teaspoons icing sugar, sifted
250 g/9 oz seedless grapes, halved,
  or black grapes, halved and
  seeded
10 ratafia biscuits, crushed
extra ratafias (optional)

1 Heat the oven to 190C/375F/Gas 5. Grease a 33 × 23 cm/13 × 9 inch Swiss roll tin; line tin with grease-proof paper and grease paper.
2 Sift the flour with the salt and baking powder and set aside.
3 Put the eggs and sugar into a large heatproof bowl. Set the bowl over a pan half full of gently simmering water. ! Using a rotary or hand-held electric whisk, beat the mixture until thick and foamy. Continue beating until the mixture is thick enough to hold the trail of the whisk for about 3 seconds when beaters are lifted.
4 Remove the bowl from the pan and beat for a few minutes more until the mixture is cool. Using a large metal spoon, fold in the sifted flour, one-third at a time.
5 Pour mixture into the prepared baking tin and spread evenly by gently tilting the tin. Bake the cake immediately in the oven for 15-20 minutes until the surface is golden and springy to the touch. Leave to stand in the tin for 1-2 seconds, then turn out on to a wire rack. Peel off the lining paper and leave to cool completely.
6 Make filling: whip cream in a bowl with kirsch and sugar until standing in soft peaks. Spoon half the whipped cream into another bowl and fold in three-quarters of the prepared grapes.
7 Assemble gâteau: cut sponge across into 3 equal rectangles, then sandwich them together with the grape cream in between. Spread three-quarters of the remaining whipped cream over the top and sides. Transfer to a serving plate.
8 Using a palette knife, press the crushed ratafias over the sides of the gâteau. Put the remaining cream into a piping bag fitted with a large star nozzle and pipe a border around the top edge. Decorate with the remaining grapes and the ratafias, if liked. Keep in a cool place and serve within 2 hours.

Cook's Notes

TIME
35-40 minutes, plus cooling and assembling.

WATCHPOINT
If using an electric table mixer there is no need to place bowl over hot water. If beating over hot water, check that the bottom of the bowl does not touch the water or the eggs will scramble.

●480 calories/500 kj per slice

Chestnut cream gâteau

MAKES 8-10 SLICES
3 large eggs, separated
75 g/3 oz caster sugar
75 g/3 oz plain flour, sifted
1 tablespoon water
vegetable oil, for greasing
caster sugar, for coating

FILLING AND DECORATION
250 g/9 oz can chestnut spread
300 ml/½ pint double cream
1 tablespoon brandy
marrons glacés, sliced, to decorate

1 Heat the oven to 190C/375F/Gas 5. Lightly grease two 20 cm/8 inch sandwich tins, line their bases with greaseproof paper, then lightly grease the paper. Lightly coat the tins with caster sugar, tipping out the excess (see Cook's tips).

2 Put the eggs and sugar in a heatproof bowl over a pan of gently simmering water, making sure that the bottom of the bowl does not touch the water (see Cook's tips). Using a rotary or hand-held electric whisk, beat until the mixture is thick enough to hold the trail of the whisk for 3-5 seconds when the beaters are lifted.

3 Remove the bowl from the pan and whisk for a few minutes more, then fold in the flour and water.

4 Divide the mixture evenly between prepared tins and spread evenly by gently tilting tins. Bake immediately in the oven for about 15 minutes, until the cakes are golden and springy to the touch.

5 Cool for 1-2 seconds, then turn out of the tins on to a wire rack. Peel off the lining paper and leave the cakes to cool completely.

6 To serve: cut each cake in half horizontally with a long serrated knife. Whip cream until standing in soft peaks, then fold in the chestnut spread and brandy. Use one third of the cream mixture to sandwich the cake layers together. Spread half the remaining cream mixture over the top and sides of the cake, so that they are coated completely.

7 Spoon remaining cream mixture into a piping bag fitted with a star nozzle and pipe a decorative pattern on the top of the cake. Decorate with slices of marrons glacés. Refrigerate until required.

Cook's Notes

 TIME
Preparation (including baking and cooling) takes about 1½ hours.

 COOK'S TIPS
Sugaring the cake tins makes it much easier to remove the baked sponge.
If using an electric table-top mixer, there is no need to beat over hot water.

 VARIATION
Use rum instead of brandy and maraschino cherries instead of sliced marrons glacés.

● 360 calories/1500 kj per slice

Celebration cake

MAKES 35-40 SLICES

1.5 kg/3 lb 4 oz mixed dried fruit
100 g/4 oz glacé cherries, halved
100 g/4 oz shelled walnuts, chopped
500 g/1 lb plain flour
1 tablespoon ground mixed spice
pinch of salt
350 g/12 oz margarine or butter
350 g/12 oz light soft brown sugar
7 eggs
grated zest and juice of 1 lemon
grated zest and juice of 1 orange
3 tablespoons brandy
750 g/1½ lb almond marzipan
4 tablespoons apricot jam, sieved
    and warmed
margarine, for greasing

FONDANT ICING

1 egg white
2 tablespoons liquid glucose
1 teaspoon lemon juice
500 g/1 lb icing sugar, sifted
few drops of yellow food colouring
extra icing sugar and a little
    cornflour, for dusting

DECORATIVE ICING

1 egg white
225 g/8 oz icing sugar, sifted
few drops of yellow food colouring

1 Heat the oven to 170C/325F/Gas 3. Grease and line the sides and base of a 23 cm/9 inch square cake tin with a double thickness of greaseproof paper. Grease the paper.
2 Mix the dried fruit, glacé cherries and walnuts in a bowl. Sift the flour with the spice and salt into a separate bowl, then add half the flour to the fruit and mix well.
3 Beat margarine and sugar until pale. Gradually beat in eggs adding a little flour with each. Fold in remaining flour.
4 Stir in fruits, citrus zest and juice. Turn into tin, level and make shallow hollow in centre.
5 Bake in oven for 3½-4 hours or until a warmed fine skewer inserted in centre comes out clean. Leave to cool for 30 minutes. Prick top and spoon on brandy. Leave until cold.
6 Turn out, peel off the greaseproof paper, wrap in foil and store in an airtight tin for at least 2 months.

7 Eight days before the cake is required, prepare the marzipan covering: brush the cake all over with warm apricot jam. Sift a little icing sugar over a work surface and roll out half the marzipan to a 24 cm/9½ inch square. Press on to cake top and trim edges.
8 Roll the remaining marzipan to a 30 × 23 cm/12 × 9 inch rectangle. Cut into 4 strips across and press a piece on to each side of the cake. Trim and work edges together.
9 Lift on to a 28 cm/11 inch square cake board. Leave for 7 days.
10 The day before the cake is required, make the fondant icing: put the egg white, glucose and lemon juice in a bowl. Beat in the sugar, 1 tablespoon at a time, until it is too stiff to stir, then knead to a smooth paste, adding more sugar as necessary. Work in food colouring.
11 Sift a little icing sugar over a work surface and roll out icing to a 30 cm/12 inch square. Place on the cake and, using hands dusted with cornflour, ease down the sides.
12 While the icing is still soft, mark a line 1 cm/½ inch in from the edge all the way round the top. Mark another line along the sides 1 cm/½ inch down from the edge, and another line 1 cm/½ inch up from the base. Set aside.
13 To make the decorative icing: beat the egg white until frothy, then

stir in the icing sugar, 1 tablespoon at a time. Beat until the icing forms soft peaks. Stir in food colouring.
14 Spoon the icing into a piping bag fitted with a small plain nozzle. Using the marked lines as a guide, pipe lines vertically over the edge of each side and more lines down to the base and out on to the board.
15 Pipe a dot on both ends of each line. Squeeze a dot of icing on to the back of cake decorations (see Buying guide) and fit on to each corner and in centre, then pipe 2 lines at right angles in each corner. Decorate with more dots on top of cake and on board. Dry overnight, add ribbon.

Cook's Notes

 TIME
4-4½ hours preparing cake plus storing; 20 minutes covering with marzipan, then 1 week drying; 5 hours icing, plus drying out.

BUYING GUIDE
Buy iced cake decorations from cake shops.

COOK'S TIP
Practise piping on a plate first.

● 500 calories/2100 kj per slice

Orange ring cake

MAKES 12 SLICES
175 g/6 oz self-raising flour
1 teaspoon baking powder
175 g/6 oz margarine, at room
  temperature
175 g/6 oz light soft brown sugar
3 eggs
finely grated zest of 1 orange
vegetable oil, for greasing

ICING AND DECORATION
275 g/10 oz icing sugar
finely grated zest of 1 orange
3 tablespoons orange juice
25 g/1 oz plain dessert chocolate,
  broken into pieces
thin slices of orange (optional)

1 Heat the oven to 180C/350F/Gas 4.
Thoroughly grease a 1.5 L/2½ pint
(23 cm/9 inch) plain ring mould.
2 Sift the flour and baking powder
into a large bowl. Add the margarine, sugar, eggs and orange zest,
then beat with a wooden spoon for
2-3 minutes until blended (see
Cook's tips).
3 Turn the mixture into the prepared mould and level the surface.
Bake in the oven for 35-40 minutes,
until a warmed fine skewer inserted
into the centre comes out clean.
4 Cool the cake for 3 minutes, then
run a palette knife around the sides
to loosen it and turn out of the tin
on to a wire rack. Leave the cake to
cool completely.
5 Make the icing: sift the icing
sugar into a bowl. Add the orange
zest and juice and mix with a
wooden spoon until blended.
6 Place a large plate underneath the
wire rack. Pour icing over top of
cake and quickly spread it over the
sides with a palette knife. Leave the
icing to set. [!]
7 Put the chocolate into a heatproof
bowl over a pan of barely simmering water. Heat gently until melted,
stirring occasionally.
8 Put the melted chocolate into a
greaseproof paper piping bag (see
Cook's tips). Snip off the tip of the
bag and pipe squiggly lines of
chocolate over the iced cake. Leave
to set. Just before serving, arrange
orange slices in the centre, if liked.

Cook's Notes

TIME
The cake takes about 1
hour to make and bake.
Allow extra time for cooling and
about 20 minutes for icing and
decorating, plus setting.

COOK'S TIPS
You can use a hand-
held electric beater in-
stead of a wooden spoon, but
do not beat for longer than 1½-2
minutes. It is important not to
over-beat an all-in-one mixture,
or the cake will rise unevenly
and will have a heavy texture.
  If you do not want to make a
greaseproof paper bag, drizzle
the chocolate over the cake from
a metal spoon.

WATCHPOINT
Do not be tempted to
transfer the cake to a
serving plate until both icing
and decoration are set, or the
icing will crack and the look of
the cake will be spoilt.

●340 calories/1425 kj per slice

Walnut coffee cake

MAKES 8-10 SLICES
175 g/6 oz self-raising flour
175 g/6 oz caster sugar
100 g/4 oz soft tub margarine
1 heaped teaspoon instant coffee
    powder, dissolved in 1
    tablespoon boiling water
3 tablespoons milk
2 large eggs, beaten
75 g/3 oz chopped walnuts
vegetable oil, for greasing
walnut halves, for decoration

SYRUP
75 g/3 oz caster sugar
4 tablespoons water
1 teaspoon instant coffee powder
7.5 cm/3 inch stick cinnamon

1 Heat the oven to 180C/350F/Gas 4.
Grease a 1.75 L/3 pint loaf tin, then
line the base with non-stick
parchment paper.
2 Sift the flour into a bowl. Add the
sugar, margarine, coffee, milk and
eggs. Mix well with a wooden
spoon, then beat for 2-3 minutes,
until blended. Using a large metal
spoon, fold in the walnuts.
3 Turn the mixture into the
prepared tin and level the surface.
Bake in the oven for 55-60 minutes,
or until springy to the touch.
4 Make the syrup: gently heat the
sugar with the water, coffee powder
and cinnamon stick until the sugar
is dissolved. Bring slowly to the
boil, then remove from the heat and
keep hot. Remove and discard the
cinnamon stick.
5 Run a round-bladed knife around
the edges of the cake to loosen it.
Prick the top with a fine skewer,
then spoon the hot syrup over the
whole surface.
6 Leave the cake to cool completely,
then turn out of the tin and carefully
peel off the lining paper. ✳ Place
the cake, the right way up, on a
serving dish and decorate with
walnut halves.

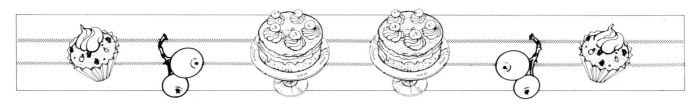

Spinning top cake

MAKES 16 SLICES
225 g/8 oz self-raising flour
1 teaspoon baking powder
225 g/8 oz margarine, softened
225 g/8 oz caster sugar
4 eggs
few drops of pink food colouring
4-5 tablespoons raspberry jam
margarine, for greasing

ICING
225 g/8 oz butter, softened
500 g/1 lb icing sugar, sifted
25 g/1 oz desiccated coconut
few drops each of pink, green and
orange food colouring

1 Heat the oven to 180C/350F/Gas 4.
2 Fully grease two 20 cm/8 inch sandwich tins, line them with greaseproof paper. Grease the paper.
3 Sift flour and baking powder into

a large bowl, add the margarine, sugar and eggs and then beat with a hand-held electric mixer for 1 minute or with a wooden spoon for 2 minutes.
4 Divide the mixture equally into 2 and stir pink colouring into one half. Put mixture into prepared tins in alternate spoonfuls of plain and pink mixture.
5 Bake in oven for 30-35 minutes or until it is golden brown and springy to the touch.
6 Turn the cakes out on to a wire rack and leave to cool completely.
7 Sandwich the cooled cakes together with jam.
8 Make the icing: put the butter into a bowl and beat in the icing sugar a little at a time. Place one-third of icing in a separate bowl. Soften with a little warm water and spread around sides of the cake.
9 Spread out the coconut on a piece of greaseproof paper. Hold the top and bottom of the cake firmly between both hands and then roll sides of the cake in the coconut until

Cook's Notes

TIME
30 minutes preparation and 30-35 minutes cooking, plus cooling. Icing the cake takes about 20 minutes.

VARIATION
Instead of a rough icing, pipe rosettes of different-coloured icing.

● 475 calories/2000 kj per slice

evenly coated. Place the cake on a serving plate.
10 Put 4 tablespoons of icing in a separate bowl and add a few drops of pink colouring. Repeat with green and orange colouring. Leave the rest of the icing plain.
11 Mark the cake into 8 sections and rough ice in different colours. Pipe plain icing round top and base of the spinning top cake. Serve on day it is iced.

Chocolate peppermint gâteau

MAKES 20 SLICES

100 g/4 oz plain chocolate
300 ml/½ pint milk
225 g/8 oz light soft brown sugar
100 g/4 oz soft-tub margarine
2 eggs, separated
225 g/8 oz plain flour
1 teaspoon bicarbonate of soda
margarine, for greasing

ICING AND DECORATION

100 g/4 oz butter or margarine,
  softened
225 g/8 oz icing sugar, sifted
few drops of green food colouring
few drops of peppermint
  flavouring
2-3 tablespoons water
75 g/3 oz chocolate vermicelli
4 wafer-thin peppermint
  chocolates, cut diagonally in half
25 g/1 oz plain chocolate, grated

1 Heat the oven to 170C/325F/Gas 3. Grease a deep 20 cm/8 inch square cake tin, line with greaseproof paper and grease the paper.
2 Break the chocolate into a small bowl set over a pan of simmering water. Add half the milk and half the sugar. ⚠ When the chocolate has melted, remove from the heat and gently stir in the remaining milk and mix well.
3 Beat the fat and remaining sugar in a bowl with the egg yolks. Beat in the chocolate mixture, then sift in the flour and bicarbonate of soda. Mix until well blended, then beat for 1 minute.
4 In a clean dry bowl, whisk the egg whites until standing in stiff peaks. Then, using a metal spoon, carefully fold 1 tablespoon into the mixture, then fold in the rest of the egg white.
5 Turn mixture into prepared tin and smooth the top with a palette knife. Bake in the oven for 1-1¼ hours, until the cake springs back when lightly pressed. Turn on to a wire rack, remove the lining paper, turn the cake the right way up and leave to cool.
6 Meanwhile, make peppermint icing: beat butter until it is soft and creamy. Gradually beat in the icing sugar, green colouring, peppermint flavouring and enough water to give a smooth buttercream which will hold its shape.
7 Spread one-third of the icing round the sides of the cake. Spread the vermicelli out on a piece of greaseproof paper then, holding the cake firmly in both hands, dip it in the vermicelli until the sides are completely coated.
8 Put the cake on a serving plate. Spread half the remaining icing over the top of the cake then, using a piping bag with a large rosette nozzle, pipe the rest in a border around the edge of the cake. Arrange the peppermint chocolate halves in the piped icing and then sprinkle the grated plain chocolate over the centre of the cake, for an attractive decoration.

Raspberry cream cake

MAKES 6-8 SLICES

100 g/4 oz self-raising flour
1 teaspoon baking powder
100 g/4 oz soft tub margarine
100 g/4 oz caster sugar
2 large eggs, beaten
1-2 drops vanilla essence
melted margarine, for greasing

FILLING

150 ml/¼ pint whipping cream
100 g/4 oz raspberries, well drained
  if canned (see Cook's tip),
  defrosted if frozen
4-6 tablespoons raspberry jam
icing sugar, to dredge

1 Heat the oven to 170C/325F/Gas 3. Grease the bases of two 18 cm/7 inch round sandwich tins and line them with greaseproof paper; grease the lining paper.
2 Sift the flour and baking powder into a large bowl. Add the soft margarine, caster sugar, eggs and vanilla essence and beat vigorously for 2-3 minutes until blended.
3 Divide the mixture equally between the prepared tins, level each surface and make a shallow hollow in the centre. Bake in the oven for 25 minutes until just firm to the touch.
4 Let the cakes stand in the tins for a few minutes before turning out on a rack (see Preparation). Peel off lining paper. Turn cakes the right way up, then leave to cool completely.

5 Make the filling: whip the cream until stiff. Lightly crush the raspberries and fold them into the whipped cream.
6 Spread 1 cake with half the jam, then with the raspberry cream filling. Spread the underside of the other cake evenly with the remaining jam. Cut it into 6-8 wedges, then position these one at a time, jam-side-down, on top of the raspberry filling (see Preparation). Sift icing sugar thickly over the top.

Cook's Notes

TIME
This cake takes about 1½ hours to make.

COOK'S TIP
A 200 g/7 oz can raspberries will give 100 g/4 oz drained raspberries.

PREPARATION
To prevent their delicate surface being marked, lay a clean tea-towel on the wire rack before turning out the cakes.

Place the cake wedges jam-side-down and slightly apart so that the cream filling shows through. Cut a thin strip off the last wedge of cake or it will not fit.

FREEZING
Wrap the cold cakes separately, or with waxed paper between them; freeze for up to 6 months. Defrost for 1-2 hours.

●405 calories/1700 kj per slice

Ginger layer cake

MAKES 6-8 SLICES
100 g/4 oz self-raising flour
1 teaspoon baking powder
100 g/4 oz soft tub margarine
100 g/4 oz caster sugar
2 large eggs, beaten
melted margarine or butter, for greasing

FILLING AND DECORATION
150 ml/¼ pint whipping cream
8 tablespoons ginger marmalade
2 gingernut biscuits, coarsely crushed (optional)

1 Heat the oven to 170C/325F/Gas 3. Grease two 18 cm/7 inch round sandwich tins, line each base with greaseproof paper, then grease the paper.
2 Sift the flour and baking powder into a large bowl. Add the margarine, sugar and eggs and beat together with a wooden spoon for 2-3 minutes.
3 Divide the mixture equally between the prepared tins, level each surface and make a shallow hollow in the centre. Bake in the oven for 25 minutes until springy to the touch.
4 Cool the cakes for a few minutes, then turn out of the tins and carefully peel off the lining paper. Leave, the right way up, on a wire rack to cool completely.
5 Cut each cake in half horizontally to make 4 layers altogether (see Preparation). Whip the cream until standing in soft peaks.
6 Assemble the cake: spread 1 layer with half the marmalade, place another layer on top and spread with half the cream. Top with another layer and spread with the remaining marmalade. Place the last layer, cut side down, on top and spread with the rest of the cream. Sprinkle the crushed gingernuts around the top edge, if using. Serve within 1 hour, or chill in the refrigerator.

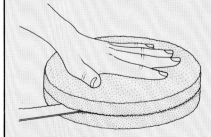

Frosted walnut cake

MAKES 8 SLICES

100 g/4 oz self-raising flour
pinch of salt
100 g/4 oz margarine or butter
100 g/4 oz caster sugar
2 eggs, beaten
50 g/2 oz walnuts, finely chopped
melted margarine or vegetable oil,
    for greasing

MERINGUE FROSTING
    (see Did you know)
175 g/6 oz caster sugar
pinch of salt
pinch of cream of tartar
2 tablespoons water
1 egg white
few drops of vanilla flavouring
8 walnut halves, to decorate

1 Heat the oven to 180C/350F/Gas 4. Grease two 18 cm/7 inch sandwich tins. Line each base with grease-proof paper, then grease the paper.
2 Sift the flour and salt into a bowl and set aside. Beat the margarine and sugar together until pale and fluffy, then beat in the eggs, a little at a time (see Cook's tips). Using a large metal spoon, fold in the sifted flour and chopped walnuts.
3 Divide the mixture equally between the prepared tins and level the surface. Bake in the oven, just above the centre, for about 25 minutes, until golden and springy to the touch.
4 Leave in the tins for 3 minutes, then turn out on to a wire rack and peel off the lining paper. Turn the cakes the right way up and leave to cool completely (see Cook's tips).
5 Make the meringue frosting: place the sugar, salt, cream of tartar, water and egg white in a heatproof bowl and beat together with a hand-held electric whisk for 30 seconds. Set the bowl over a pan of gently simmering water ! and whisk at high speed for 5-7 minutes, until the frosting stands in peaks when the beaters are lifted out of the mixture. Remove the bowl from the pan and whisk in the vanilla flavouring.
6 Place 1 cake on a serving plate and spread with a little of the frosting. Put the remaining cake on top. Working quickly, pile the frosting on top of the cake and spread it over the top and sides with a palette knife, then mark it into decorative swirls. ! Before the frosting sets, gently press the walnut halves on to the top of the cake. Leave to set before serving.

Raspberry layer cake

MAKES 6-8 SLICES

225 g/8 oz plain flour
4 teaspoons baking powder
¼ teaspoon salt
75 g/ 3 oz butter or margarine, diced
75 g/3 oz caster sugar
1 egg, beaten
3 tablespoons milk
extra butter, for greasing

TO FINISH
500 g/1 lb raspberries
75 g/3 oz caster sugar
150 ml/¼ pint whipping cream

1 Heat the oven to 190C/375F/Gas 5. Grease a loose-based, deep 20 cm/ 8 inch round cake tin.

2 Make the cake: sift the flour, baking powder and salt into a bowl. Add the butter and rub it in with your fingertips until the mixture resembles breadcrumbs. Stir in the sugar, then make a well in the centre. Add the egg and 2 tablespoons milk and mix with a fork to a soft scone-like dough, adding remaining milk if necessary.

3 Turn the dough out on to a lightly floured surface and knead briefly, then pat out to a round. Place in the prepared tin and press gently to fit the base. Bake above centre of oven for 25 minutes, or until well risen and golden brown.

4 Cool the cake for 5 minutes, then remove from the tin and place on a wire rack. Using a serrated knife, cut the cake horizontally in half. Separate the halves and leave to cool completely.

5 Meanwhile, reserve 6-8 whole raspberries to decorate the cake. Place the remaining berries in a bowl and crush lightly. Sprinkle over the sugar and mix gently. Cover and reserve until required.

6 To serve: stir the crushed raspberries, then spoon half over each of the cold layers of the cake. Transfer the bottom layer to a serving plate. Place the remaining layer, raspberry side up, on top. Whip the cream until standing in soft peaks, then pipe or spoon around top edge of cake. Decorate with the reserved raspberries and serve as soon as possible (see Cook's tip).

Cook's Notes

 TIME
15-20 minutes preparation and 25 minutes baking, plus cooling. Finishing takes about 15 minutes.

 COOK'S TIP
The layer cake should be finished and served on the day of making as it dries out and becomes stale quickly.

 VARIATIONS
To make individual cakes, divide the kneaded dough into 8 equal pieces and shape each into a 6.5 cm/2½ inch round. Place on greased baking sheet and bake for about 12-15 minutes, until well risen and golden brown. Split, cool and finish as for the large layer cake.

Other fruits make a delicious layer cake. Try strawberries, blackberries, or skinned, cored and chopped fresh pineapple.

●450 calories/1875 kj per slice

Simnel cake

SERVES 16

225 g/8 oz plain flour
1 teaspoon ground cinnamon
1 teaspoon ground mixed spice
½ teaspoon freshly grated nutmeg
pinch of salt
350 g/12 oz currants
175 g/6 oz sultanas
100 g/4 oz cut mixed peel
175 g/6 oz butter, softened
175 g/6 oz dark soft brown sugar
3 large eggs, lightly beaten
750 g/1½ lb almond marzipan
icing sugar, for dusting
sieved and warmed apricot jam
vegetable oil, for greasing

1 Heat the oven to 150C/300F/Gas 2. Grease a deep, 18 cm/7 inch round tin, line base and sides with double thickness greaseproof paper, then grease the paper.
2 Sift flour, spices and salt into a bowl. In a separate bowl, mix the dried fruits and peel. Reserve.
3 Beat butter and brown sugar until pale and fluffy. Beat in eggs, a little at a time. Fold in sifted flour alternately with the fruit mixture.
4 Sprinkle work surface with icing sugar, then roll out one-third of marzipan to an 18 cm/7 inch circle.
5 Put half the cake mixture into prepared tin and level the surface. Press marzipan circle gently on top. Spoon over remaining cake mixture.
6 Bake in oven for about 3 hours, until well browned and firm to the touch. (Cover with greaseproof paper if browning too fast.) Cool cake for 30 minutes, then turn out of tin and peel off lining paper. Leave on a wire rack to cool completely. Wrap in cling film or foil and store in an airtight container, in a cool place for at least 1 week.
7 To decorate: sprinkle work surface with icing sugar, then roll out half remaining marzipan to an 18 cm/7 inch circle. Brush top of cake with jam, then cover with marzipan circle and press in place. Crimp edges then brush surface with jam.
8 Heat the grill to moderate.
9 Use remaining marzipan to make 11 equal-sized balls and stick around top edge of cake. Grill until browned. ⌐!⌐ Cool completely.

Cook's Notes

TIME
40 minutes preparation, 3 hours baking, plus cooling, storing and decorating.

WATCHPOINT
Watch the cake constantly while it is under the grill and turn it round, if necessary, to ensure that the marzipan browns as evenly as possible and does not burn.

DID YOU KNOW
In England, this cake was associated with Mothering Sunday when girls in service were given a holiday and would take the cake home as a gift. Today the Simnel cake is usually baked for Easter Sunday. The marzipan balls are thought to represent the 11 faithful Apostles. The cake can be finished with glacé or marzipan fruits or bought decorations and a ribbon.

● 495 calories/2050 kj per slice

Sherry layer cake

MAKES 10-12 SLICES

175 g/6 oz self-raising flour
175 g/6 oz caster sugar
175 g/6 oz margarine (see Buying guide)
3 eggs
finely grated zest of 1 orange
2 tablespoons sweet sherry
2 tablespoons orange juice
extra margarine, for greasing

SHERRY BUTTER ICING
75 g/3 oz butter, softened
225 g/8 oz icing sugar, sifted
2 tablespoons sweet sherry
frosted flowers (see Preparation)

1 Heat the oven to 180C/350F/Gas 4. Grease two 4 cm/1½ inch deep, 18 cm/7 inch round tins. Line each base with greaseproof paper, then lightly grease the paper.

2 Sift the flour into a large bowl. Add the sugar, margarine, eggs and orange zest and beat with a wooden spoon for 2-3 minutes until evenly and smoothly blended.

3 Divide the mixture between the prepared tins and level each surface. Stand the tins on a baking sheet, then bake in the oven for 35-40 minutes, or until the cakes are springy to the touch.

4 Cool the cakes for 1-2 minutes, then turn out of the tins and peel off the lining paper. Place the cakes, the right way up, on a wire rack and leave to cool completely.

5 Make the icing: beat the butter until very soft, then slowly beat in the icing sugar. Continue beating until the mixture is pale and creamy, then beat in the sherry.

6 Assemble the cake: place 1 cake on a serving plate. Mix together the sherry and orange juice and spoon half evenly over cake. Spread one-third of the icing over the cake, then top with the second cake. Sprinkle with the remaining sherry and orange mixture. Spread top with half of remaining icing, leaving a 5 mm/¼ inch border around the edge. Mark a wavy pattern in the topping with a small palette knife.

7 Place remaining icing in a piping bag fitted with a small star nozzle and pipe a border of small rosettes around top edge of cake. Refrigerate for 20-25 minutes to firm. Just before serving, decorate with frosted flowers.

Cook's Notes

TIME
10 minutes preparation and 35-40 minutes baking for the cakes. Cooling takes about 1 hour (during which time the flowers can be frosted). Assembling and decorating the cake takes 20 minutes.

BUYING GUIDE
For the best possible results, use block margarine at room temperature. Soft tub margarine is not suitable for this all-in-one mix as it easily over-creams.

PREPARATION
Choose small, non-poisonous and colourful fresh flowers: primulas, small pansies, violets, cherry and apple blossom are all suitable. Wash and dry flowers, then brush with lightly beaten egg white. Sprinkle with caster sugar and leave 15 minutes to dry completely.

The flowers are for decoration only and are not intended to be eaten.

●460 calories/1925 kj per portion

Almond slices

MAKES 16

215 g/7½ oz shortcrust pastry, defrosted if frozen
2 large egg whites
150 g/5 oz ground almonds
150 g/5 oz caster sugar
2-3 drops almond flavouring
100 g/4 oz red jam
50 g/2 oz flaked almonds
icing sugar, to dust (optional)

1 Heat the oven to 180C/350F/Gas 4.
2 Roll out the pastry on a lightly floured surface to a rectangle, about 30 × 20 cm/12 × 8 inches. Loosely roll the pastry around the rolling pin, then unroll it over a 28 × 18 cm/11 × 7 inch Swiss roll tin. Gently press the pastry over the base and up the sides of the tin, then trim off any surplus. Set aside in the refrigerator.
3 In a spotlessly clean, dry bowl, whisk the egg whites until they stand in stiff peaks. Using a large metal spoon, fold in the ground almonds, caster sugar and almond flavouring.
4 Spread the jam over the pastry base, then carefully cover with the stiff almond mixture. Scatter the flaked almonds over the top. Bake in the oven for 35 minutes until golden.
5 Leave to cool for 30 minutes, then cut into 16 slices and remove from the tin with a palette knife. Leave on a wire rack to cool completely. ✳
Just before, serving, sift a little icing sugar over the slices, if liked.

Cook's Notes

TIME
20 minutes preparation, 35 minutes baking, plus cooling time.

FREEZING
Pack in a rigid container with waxed paper between layers. Cover and freeze for up to 1 month. Defrost on a wire rack at room temperature for 1-2 hours.

STORAGE
These slices will keep for 2-3 days in an air-tight container, in a cool, dry place.

VARIATIONS
Other jams can be used —the flavour of apricot goes well with almonds.

●180 calories/750 kj per slice

American carrot cake

MAKES 16 PIECES
100 g/4 oz plain flour
1 teaspoon bicarbonate of soda
1 teaspoon ground cinnamon
½ teaspoon salt
225 g/8 oz light soft brown sugar
175 ml/6 fl oz vegetable oil
2 large eggs
175 g/6 oz carrots, grated (see Cook's tip)
extra oil, for greasing

FROSTING
75 g/3 oz Philadelphia cheese
25 g/1 oz butter, softened
100 g/4 oz caster sugar
1 canned pineapple ring, drained thoroughly and finely chopped (optional)
few drops of vanilla flavouring

1 Heat the oven to 180C/350F/Gas 4. Lightly oil a 5 cm/2 inch deep, 18 cm/7 inch square cake tin, line sides and base with grease-proof paper, then oil the paper.
2 Sift the flour with the soda, the cinnamon and salt and reserve.

3 Put the sugar into a large bowl. Using an electric whisk, gradually whisk in the oil. Beat in the eggs, one at a time. Add the flour mixture and mix with a wooden spoon until evenly blended, then stir in the carrots, mixing well.
4 Pour mixture into prepared cake tin and bake in the oven for 1 hour 10 minutes, until risen and firm to the touch at the centre. (The top will probably crack slightly.) Cover with greaseproof paper halfway through baking time to avoid overbrowning.

5 Cool the cake for 5 minutes, then turn out of the tin on to a wire rack. Peel off the lining paper and leave to cool completely.
6 Make the frosting: put the cheese into a large bowl with the butter, sugar, vanilla and the pineapple, if using, and beat until well blended.
7 Turn the cake the right way up and place on a large serving plate. Spread the frosting over the top. To serve: cut the cake into quarters, then cut each quarter into 4 squares (see Storage).

Chocolate marble cake

MAKES 10 SLICES

175 g/6 oz butter or margarine,
    softened
175 g/6 oz caster sugar
3 eggs, lightly beaten
75 g/3 oz plain flour
75 g/3 oz self-raising flour
1 tablespoon cocoa powder
1 tablespoon vanilla flavouring
extra butter, for greasing
2 tablespoons ground almonds, for
    the tin (see Cook's tips)

1 Heat the oven to 180C/350F/Gas 4.
2 Butter a 1.6 L/2¾ pint (1 kg/2 lb)
metal loaf tin, then sprinkle in the
almonds. Tip and tilt tin until base
and sides are evenly coated, then
invert and tap the base gently to
remove any excess.
3 Beat the butter and sugar until
pale and fluffy. Add the eggs a little
at a time, beating thoroughly after
each addition. Sift the flours

together and fold into the mixture
with a large metal spoon.
4 Divide the mixture into 2 separate
halves. Sift the cocoa into one half
and lightly fold it in, then stir the
vanilla into the other half.
5 Spread half the vanilla mixture in
prepared tin and level the surface.
Cover with half the cocoa mixture.
Spread the rest of vanilla mixture
evenly on top, then finish with a
layer of the remaining cocoa mixture (see Cook's tips).

6 Bake cake in oven for about 50
minutes, until a warmed fine skewer inserted into the centre comes
out clean. (Cover tin with greaseproof paper after 30 minutes baking
time to prevent the top of the cake
overbrowning.)
7 Cool the cake for 2-3 minutes,
then run a palette knife around the
sides and turn out of the tin. Turn
the right way up and leave on a
wire rack to cool completely before
slicing and serving (see Storage).

Cook's Notes

TIME
30 minutes preparation
and 50 minutes baking.
Allow 2-3 hours for cooling.

COOK'S TIPS
Coating the tin gives
cake a light crust and
avoids need for lining paper.
  There is no need to draw a
skewer through the mixture;
the layers swirl together as the
cake rises during baking.

WATCHPOINT
Handle the cake gently
when turning it out of
the tin because it is very fragile
and can easily crack or break at
this stage.

STORAGE
The cake will keep fresh
for up to 1 week in an
airtight container.

●285 calories/1175 kj per slice

Saffron honey cake

MAKES 8 SLICES
6 saffron strands (see Buying guide)
4 tablespoons milk
175 g/6 oz plain flour
1 tablespoon baking powder
100 g/4 oz butter or margarine, softened
50 g/2 oz caster sugar
2 tablespoons clear honey
2 eggs, lightly beaten
50 g/2 oz cut mixed peel
75 g/3 oz sultanas
vegetable oil, for greasing

ICING
10 saffron strands
1 tablespoon boiling water
200 g/7 oz icing sugar
1-2 tablespoons lemon juice

1 Heat the oven to 180C/350F/Gas 4. Grease a deep 18 cm/7 inch round cake tin, line sides and base with greaseproof paper; grease paper.

2 Crush the 6 saffron strands for the cake between your fingers and put into a small, heavy-based saucepan with the milk. Bring just to the boil, then remove from heat and leave to stand for 20 minutes.
3 Sift the flour with the baking powder and reserve.
4 Beat the butter, sugar and honey until pale and fluffy. Beat in the eggs, a little at a time, adding 1 tablespoon sifted flour if mixture shows signs of curdling. Fold in the sifted flour.
5 Strain the saffron milk, then stir into cake mixture, 1 tablespoon at a time. Fold in the peel and sultanas. Turn mixture into the prepared tin and level surface.
6 Bake in oven for 65 minutes, or until a warmed fine skewer inserted into the centre comes out clean.
7 Meanwhile, put the 10 saffron strands for the icing into a small bowl with the boiling water and leave to stand until required.
8 Cool the cake for 5 minutes, then turn out of the tin and peel off the lining paper. Turn cake right way up and leave it on a wire rack to cool completely.

9 Sift the icing sugar into a large bowl and stir in 1 tablespoon lemon juice. Strain the saffron water, then stir into the icing until evenly coloured. Stir in remaining lemon juice if necessary, to give a thick pouring consistency.
10 Place a large plate under the rack. Pour icing over cake, smooth with a palette knife and leave to set before serving (see Storage).

Cook's Notes

TIME
35 minutes preparation, 65 minutes baking, plus cooling and icing.

BUYING GUIDE
Saffron strands are available from most delicatessens, supermarkets and Indian food shops.

STORAGE
Store in airtight container for up to 3 days.

●380 calories/1575 kj per slice

Apricot cream cake

MAKES 6-8 SLICES

100 g/4 oz self-raising flour
1 teaspoon baking powder
100 g/4 oz soft tub margarine
100 g/4 oz caster sugar
2 large eggs, lightly beaten
finely grated zest of ½ orange
vegetable oil, for greasing

FILLING

150 ml/¼ pint whipping cream
4-6 tablespoons apricot jam
icing sugar, for dusting

1 Heat the oven to 170C/325F/Gas 3. Lightly grease two 18 cm/7 inch sandwich tins, line each base with greaseproof paper and grease.
2 Sift the flour and baking powder into a large bowl. Add the margarine, sugar, eggs and orange zest and beat vigorously with a wooden spoon for 2-3 minutes, until smoothly and evenly blended.
3 Divide the mixture equally between the prepared tins and level each surface. Bake in the oven for about 25 minutes, until the cakes are just firm to the touch.
4 Cool the cakes for 2-3 minutes, then turn out of the tins and peel off the lining papers. Leave the cakes, the right way up, on a wire rack to cool completely (see Storage).
5 Assemble the cake: whip the cream until standing in soft peaks. Place 1 cake on a serving plate (see Cook's tip) and spread with the jam and then the whipped cream. Place the other cake on top. Sift icing sugar over the top and serve as soon as possible.

Cook's Notes

TIME
The cake takes about 1¾ hours to make, bake, cool and assemble.

SPECIAL OCCASION
Flavour the cream for the filling with 2-3 teaspoons orange-flavoured liqueur. Decorate the top of the cake with piped cream, drained canned apricot halves and angelica (as shown in the photograph).

STORAGE
Wrap each cake in cling film and keep in an air-tight container for up to 3 days.

COOK'S TIP
Choose the best look-ing, most even cake for the top layer. If the other cake is lopsided, trim it level or place it upside down on the plate so that the flat base is uppermost.

● 405 calories/1700 kj per slice

Old-fashioned seed cake

MAKES 12 SLICES

100 g/4 oz plain flour
100 g/4 oz self-raising flour
pinch of salt
175 g/6 oz butter, softened
175 g/6 oz caster sugar
3 large eggs, lightly beaten
2 tablespoons milk
2 teaspoons caraway seeds
2 tablespoons sugar, to finish
vegetable oil, for greasing

1 Heat the oven to 170C/325F/Gas 3. Grease a 1.75 L/3 pint (1 kg/2 lb) loaf tin. Line the tin with greaseproof paper, then grease the paper.
2 Sift the flours with the salt.
3 In a separate bowl, beat the butter and sugar until very pale and fluffy. Add the eggs, a little at a time, beating the mixture thoroughly after each addition.
4 Using a large metal spoon, fold in the sifted flours, then stir in milk. Add the caraway seeds and gently fold them in, making sure they are evenly distributed. Turn the mixture into the prepared tin and level the surface, then make a shallow hollow in the centre. Sprinkle the sugar over the top.
5 Bake in the oven for 1-1¼ hours (see Cook's tip), or until firm to the touch and a warmed fine skewer inserted into the centre of the cake comes out clean.
6 Cool the cake for 10-15 minutes, then turn out of the tin and peel off the lining paper. Place the cake the right way up on a wire rack and then leave to cool completely before slicing and serving.

Cook's Notes

TIME
15 minutes preparation and 1¼ hours baking. Allow 2-3 hours cooling time for the cooked cake.

STORAGE
The cake (or any left-over slices) will keep for 2-3 weeks stored in an airtight container in a cool place.

COOK'S TIP
Check the cake after 1 hour's baking. Cover with greaseproof paper, if necessary, to prevent over-browning. Unlike sponges, this cake does not rise evenly, so do not worry if the top peaks and cracks slightly.

●200 calories/850 kj per slice

DID YOU KNOW
Seed cake is an old-fashioned English recipe using a Madeira mixture with caraway seeds added.
Traditionally a round cake, this variation is made in a loaf tin so that it can be cut into slices or thick finger shapes. Serve, unbuttered, with either tea or coffee.

Peaches and cream gâteau

SERVES 6

3 large eggs
75 g/3 oz light soft brown sugar
1-2 drops vanilla essence
75 g/3 oz plain flour
vegetable oil, for greasing

FILLING
150 ml/¼ pint double cream
150 ml/¼ pint single cream
1 teaspoon caster sugar
1-2 drops vanilla essence
400 g/14 oz can sliced peaches in
  syrup, well drained
15-25 g/½-1 oz flaked almonds,
  toasted, to decorate

1 Heat the oven to 190C/375F/Gas 5. Lightly brush the inside of two 18 cm/7 inch sandwich tins with oil, line their bases with greaseproof paper, then lightly oil the paper.
2 Put the eggs, sugar and vanilla essence in a large heatproof bowl. Set the bowl over a pan half full of gently simmering water. ⚠
3 Using a rotary or hand-held electric whisk, beat together until the mixture is thick and foamy. Continue until the mixture will hold the trail of the whisk for 3 seconds when the beaters are lifted.
4 Remove the bowl from the pan and whisk for a few minutes more until the mixture is cool. Sift one-third of the flour over the mixture, then fold it in with a large metal spoon. Add the remaining flour in the same way.
5 Divide the mixture equally between the prepared tins and spread evenly by gently tilting the tins. Bake the cakes immediately in the oven for 15 minutes until each is golden brown and springs back when lightly pressed in the centre.
6 Leave the baked cakes to stand in the tins for 1-2 seconds, then turn out on to a wire rack. Peel off the lining paper, turn the cakes the right way up and leave until cold. ✳
7 To serve: whip the creams together until standing in soft peaks, then quickly whisk in the sugar and vanilla. Chop the peaches, reserving 6 for decoration. Place one sponge upside down on a serving plate. Spread one-third of the cream over the cake. Scatter the chopped peaches over the cream.
8 Cover with the second sponge and spread half the remaining cream over the top. Put the rest of the cream into a piping bag fitted with a star nozzle and pipe a border of cream round the cake.
9 Arrange the reserved peach slices on the cream in the centre of the gâteau. Sprinkle flaked almonds over the top and serve within 1-2 hours.

Cook's Notes

TIME
Preparation takes 30-40 minutes, depending on type of whisk used. Baking takes 15 minutes. Allow another 20-30 minutes for the cakes to cool and 15-20 minutes for filling and decorating.

WATCHPOINT
Check that the bottom of the bowl does not touch the water during whisking or the eggs will set.

FREEZING
This type of cake is best frozen while still slightly warm—it will stay fresher and moister once defrosted. Wrap the plain cakes separately, and freeze for up to 10 months. Allow about 1 hour to defrost at room temperature then fill and decorate.

●335 calories/1400 kj per portion

Spiced marble cake

MAKES 8 SLICES
175 g/6 oz self-raising flour
175 g/6 oz soft tub margarine
175 g/6 oz caster sugar
3 eggs, beaten
½ teaspoon ground mixed spice
½ teaspoon ground cinnamon
¼ teaspoon freshly grated nutmeg
2 teaspoons black treacle (see
   Cook's tips)
2 teaspoons custard powder
melted margarine or vegetable oil,
   for greasing

FUDGE ICING
50 g/2 oz margarine or butter
50 g/2 oz dark soft brown sugar
2 tablespoons milk
75 g/3 oz icing sugar
½ teaspoon vanilla flavouring

1 Heat the oven to 170C/325F/Gas 3. Grease a deep 15 cm/6 inch round cake tin. Line the sides and base of the tin with a double thickness of greaseproof paper, then grease the paper.

2 Sift the flour into a large bowl. Add the margarine, caster sugar and eggs. Mix well with a wooden spoon, then beat for 2-3 minutes until well blended. (Or, use a hand-held electric whisk and beat for 1 minute only.)

3 Spoon one-third of the mixture into a separate bowl and thoroughly beat in the spices, treacle and custard powder.

4 Place a large spoonful of the treacle mixture in the prepared tin, followed by a large spoonful of the plain mixture. Continue in this way until both mixtures are used up. Level the surface, then make a slight hollow in the centre. Draw the blade of a knife once through the mixture, in a clockwise direction. !

5 Bake the cake in the oven for 1-1¼ hours, until a warmed fine skewer inserted in the centre comes out clean. Cool for 5 minutes, then turn out of the tin on to a wire rack. Leave to cool completely (see Cook's tips).

6 Meanwhile, make the icing: put the margarine, brown sugar and milk in a heavy-based saucepan. Stir over low heat until the margarine has melted and the sugar has dissolved, then bring slowly to the boil. Remove from the heat.

7 Sift the icing sugar into a bowl, then gradually stir in the melted mixture. Mix well, then stir in the vanilla flavouring. Leave to cool,

stirring occasionally, for about 20 minutes.

8 When the cake is cold, remove the lining paper then place the right way up on a serving plate. Beat the icing, spread it on top and mark decoratively (see Preparation).

Cook's Notes

 TIME
20-25 minutes, then 1-1¼ hours baking, plus cooling time for the cake. Allow 10 minutes, plus cooling time for the icing.

 PREPARATION
Use a round-bladed knife to spread the icing over the top of the cake. You can mark the icing in a diamond pattern as shown in the photograph or swirl it by moving the flat side of the blade in a circular direction.

 STORAGE
You can store this cake, iced or not, in an airtight container for several days. It will stay deliciously soft and moist for all this time.

 COOK'S TIPS
Warm the treacle by standing the tin in a bowl of hot water for a few minutes. This will make it easier to measure and incorporate into the cake mixture.

Because the cake is very spongy, it is best not to remove the lining paper until the cake is cold.

 WATCHPOINT
Resist the temptation to overswirl the mixture, or the marbled effect will be lost.

●470 calories/1975 kj per slice

Crispie gâteau

MAKES 6-8 SLICES

150 g/5 oz rice crispies
75 g/3 oz margarine
75 g/3 oz marshmallows
75 g/3 oz plain toffees
vegetable oil, for greasing

FILLING
½ tablespoon powdered gelatine
3 tablespoons water
600 ml/1 pint cold milk (see
    Watchpoints)
2 × 67 g/2½ oz packets butterscotch
    dessert mix
2 small bananas
1 teaspoon lemon juice
215 g/7½ oz can peach slices,
    drained

1 Lightly oil a 20 cm/8 inch
springform cake tin. Put the rice
crispies into a large bowl.
2 Put the margarine, marshmallows
and toffees into a heavy-based pan.
Heat gently, stirring occasionally,
until melted, then beat until
smooth. Pour on to the rice crispies
and mix until evenly blended.
3 With the back of a large metal
spoon press the crispie mixture
evenly over the base and sides of the
prepared tin. Leave in a cool place
for at least 2 hours to firm.
4 Make the filling: sprinkle the
gelatine over the water in a small
heatproof bowl. Leave to soak for 5
minutes, then stand bowl in a pan of
gently simmering water for 1-2
minutes, stirring occasionally, until
gelatine has dissolved. Remove
bowl from pan.
5 Pour the milk into a large bowl
and whisk in butterscotch mixes.
Leave for 1 minute until thickened,
then fold in gelatine.
6 Slice the bananas, then cut each
slice across into 3 strips. Toss in
lemon juice, then fold into butterscotch mixture. Refrigerate for 1
hour, or until on point of setting.
7 Carefully remove crispie case from
tin and place on a serving plate.
Turn butterscotch mixture into
case [!] and level the surface. Leave
in a cool place for about 1 hour, until
set. Arrange the peach slices over
the filling and serve at once.

Cook's Notes

TIME
45 minutes preparation,
plus 2 hours for the case
to firm and a further 2 hours for
the filling to set.

WATCHPOINTS
Use whole milk, or the
mixes will not thicken.
Do not assemble the gâteau
more than 1 hour before serving
or the crispie case will soften.

SERVING IDEAS
This   pudding-cum-
cake is ideal for a tea-
party; tie a ribbon around the
sides for a more festive look.

●490 calories/2050 kj per slice

BISCUITS

Party biscuit assortment

MAKES ABOUT 30
BASIC BISCUIT DOUGH
200 g/8 oz soft tub margarine
300 g/12 oz caster sugar
2 large eggs, beaten
300 g/12 oz plain flour
vegetable oil, for greasing

FLAVOURINGS
50 g/2 oz currants
2 tablespoons powdered drinking
   chocolate
grated zest of 1 lemon
¼ teaspoon lemon juice
¼ teaspoon vanilla essence

TO DECORATE
1 tablespoon caster sugar
50 g/2 oz plain chocolate
2-3 tablespoons lemon curd
2-3 tablespoons raspberry jam

1 Put the margarine and sugar into a bowl and beat together until soft and thoroughly blended. Work in the beaten eggs alternately with the flour to form a stiff dough.
2 Turn the dough on to a floured surface and cut into 4 equal pieces. Working quickly and lightly, knead the currants into the first quarter, the chocolate powder into the second, the lemon zest and juice into the third and the vanilla essence into the fourth.
3 Form each quarter of dough into a roll about 5 cm/2 inches in diameter. Wrap in foil and refrigerate for at least 30 minutes.
4 Heat the oven to 190C/375F/Gas 5. Brush 2 baking sheets with oil.
5 Remove the chocolate and currant dough from the refrigerator and cut each roll into about 8 slices, 2 mm/⅛ inch thick (see Cook's tip). Place well apart on the prepared baking sheets and bake in the oven for 10-15 minutes until just browned. Leave for 2-3 minutes, then transfer to wire racks. Sprinkle the currant biscuits with caster sugar while still warm. Leave to cool.
6 Wash and regrease the baking sheets, then remove the remaining dough from the refrigerator. Cut into slices as above. On half the vanilla biscuits, stamp out a small centre hole using a fluted cutter. Re-roll the extra dough and shape as before. Arrange on the baking sheets, then bake and cool as above.
7 To finish: melt the chocolate in a small bowl over a pan of simmering water. Dip in the chocolate biscuits so that they are half covered. Transfer to greased greaseproof paper to dry. Spread the lemon biscuits with a thin layer of lemon curd. Sandwich the vanilla biscuits together with raspberry jam, placing those with the holes on top so that the jam shows through.

Ginger shortbread

MAKES 16 FINGERS
100 g/4 oz plain flour
1½ teaspoons ground ginger
¼ teaspoon baking powder
100 g/4 oz dark soft brown sugar
100 g/4 oz medium oatmeal
finely grated zest of 1 lemon
95 g/3½ oz butter, melted
1 tablespoon golden syrup
butter, for greasing

1 Heat the oven to 170C/325F/Gas 3. Grease a 25 × 15 cm/10 × 6 inch Swiss roll tin.

2 Sift the flour, ginger and baking powder into a large bowl, then stir in the brown sugar, the oatmeal and lemon zest and mix thoroughly into the flour mixture.

3 Pour the butter and syrup into the bowl and mix lightly until the mixture is crumbly.

4 With floured hands, gather the dough together in a ball and press into the tin lightly and evenly. Prick all over with a fork, then bake in the oven for 30-40 minutes until the shortbread is golden brown.

5 Immediately cut in half lengthways, then cut into 16 fingers. Cool for 15 minutes in the tin until firm, then transfer to a serving plate and serve warm (see Serving ideas).

Cook's Notes

TIME
Preparing and cooking take 30-40 minutes.

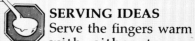

SERVING IDEAS
Serve the fingers warm with either tea or coffee. Or leave them to cool completely, then cover with whipped cream and slices of preserved ginger for an unusual mouthwatering dessert.

● 120 calories/500 kj per finger

Peanut biscuits

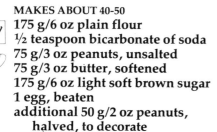

MAKES ABOUT 40-50
175 g/6 oz plain flour
½ teaspoon bicarbonate of soda
75 g/3 oz peanuts, unsalted
75 g/3 oz butter, softened
175 g/6 oz light soft brown sugar
1 egg, beaten
additional 50 g/2 oz peanuts,
**   halved, to decorate**

1 Heat the oven to 190C/375F/Gas 5. Prepare the baking sheets (see Cook's tips).
2 Sift the flour with the bicarbonate of soda.
3 Grind 75 g/3 oz peanuts in a blender or clean coffee grinder.
4 Beat the butter to a cream. Add the sugar and beat until fluffy.

5 Beat in the egg.
6 Stir in the flour and ground peanuts.
7 Form mixture into teaspoon-sized balls and then place on to the prepared baking sheets, 5 cm/2 inches apart. Flatten them slightly with a wet fork and put a half peanut in the

centre of each of the flattened shapes.
8 Bake the biscuits for 8-10 minutes. Keep a careful eye on them because they burn easily.
9 Cool them for 5 minutes on the baking sheets, then lift them with a palette knife or fish slice on to wire racks to cool completely.

Cook's Notes

 TIME
Preparation will take about 20 minutes. If you have to cook the biscuits in batches, each batch will take 15 minutes to cook and cool.

 COOK'S TIPS
Non-stick baking sheets need only be floured; others should be buttered and then floured.
    If you are baking in advance

for a party, or have some biscuits left over, store them in an airtight tin when cool.

 VARIATIONS
Use dark soft brown sugar for a stronger flavour and darker colour. If you use salted (but not dry roasted) peanuts the biscuits will taste less sweet.

● 60 calories/250 kj per portion

Oat and cherry squares

MAKES 50-60

200 g/7 oz rolled oats
50 g/2 oz plain flour
100 g/4 oz glacé cherries, chopped
100 g/4 oz margarine or butter
100 g/4 oz soft brown sugar
2 tablespoons golden syrup (see
    Cook's tip)
vegetable oil, for greasing

1 Heat the oven to 190C/375F/Gas 5. Grease a 25 × 18 cm/10 x 7 inch shallow baking tin or tray.
2 Mix the oats, flour and chopped cherries in a bowl. If the cherries stick together, separate them with your fingers, then stir them well until they are coated with the dry ingredients.
3 Put the margarine, sugar and syrup into a saucepan and stir over very low heat until the fat is melted and the sugar has dissolved. [!] Remove from the heat, pour on to the oat and cherry mixture and mix thoroughly with a large metal spoon until evenly combined.
4 Spoon the mixture into the greased tin and press evenly over the base, making sure the corners are filled. Bake in the oven for 20 minutes or until golden.
5 While the mixture is still warm, cut it into 2.5 cm/1 inch squares; lift on to a wire rack [!] and leave to cool completely (see Variation).

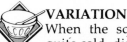

Cook's Notes

⏰ TIME
The squares take about 1½ hours to prepare, bake and cool.

[!] WATCHPOINTS
Be patient when melting the margarine, sugar and syrup: do not be tempted to speed up the process by raising the heat or the mixture is likely to become unmanageable and toffee-like.

Use a knife to loosen the squares before lifting them on to a wire rack; transfer them carefully as they will still be very soft at this stage. As the squares cool they become firm and chewy in texture.

STORAGE
These squares keep well in an airtight tin for 3-4 days.

VARIATION
When the squares are quite cold, dip each one in melted chocolate so that half of it is coated. Place on waxed paper and leave to set until completely cold.

COOK'S TIP
To measure the syrup first dip the spoon in hot water. The syrup will then slide off easily.

● 40 calories/175 kj per square

Chocolate whirls

MAKES 20-22

175 g/6 oz self-raising flour
25 g/1 oz cocoa powder
175 g/6 oz margarine, softened
50 g/2 oz icing sugar, sifted
¼ teaspoon vanilla flavouring
vegetable oil, for greasing

TO FINISH
20-24 toasted skinned hazelnut
    kernels (See Buying guide)
caster sugar (optional)

1 Heat the oven to 170C/325F/Gas 3. Grease 3 large baking sheets.
2 Sift the flour with the cocoa and reserve. In a large bowl, beat the margarine and icing sugar together until pale and creamy. Beat in the flour mixture, a little at a time, then beat in the vanilla.
3 Put the mixture into a piping bag fitted with a large star nozzle and pipe about seven 5 cm/2 inch circles on to each prepared baking sheet. Space each circle well apart to allow for spreading.
4 Place a hazelnut in the centre of each circle, then bake in the oven for 15-20 minutes, until set. Swap the baking sheets just above and just below the centre shelf half way during baking to ensure even cooking.
5 Cool the biscuits for 1-2 minutes. Using a palette knife, loosen each biscuit and transfer to wire racks. ! Dust with caster sugar, if liked.

Cook's Notes

TIME
30-40 minutes preparation (including baking), plus cooling time.

WATCHPOINT
These biscuits are very 'short' and crumbly. Use your thumb to slide them gently off the palette knife on to the rack. Do not pull them or they will break.

BUYING GUIDE
Good supermarkets sell packets of ready-toasted and skinned hazelnut kernels.

●110 calories/450 kj per whirl

Moon crescents

MAKES 36

100 g/4 oz shelled hazelnuts,
    toasted and skinned
150 g/5 oz plain flour
large pinch of salt
100 g/4 oz butter, at room
    temperature
100 g/4 oz caster sugar
2 teaspoons lemon juice
½ teaspoon vanilla flavouring
icing sugar, for dusting

1 Grind the nuts finely in a nut mill, electric coffee grinder or food processor. Sift the flour with the salt. Reserve the nuts and flour, placing them in separate bowls.
2 Beat the butter and caster sugar until very pale and fluffy, then beat in 2 teaspoons lemon juice and the vanilla. Beat in the ground nuts, one-third at a time.
3 Using a fork, gradually stir in the flour, then draw the mixture together with your fingers and work to a soft dough. Wrap in cling film and refrigerate for 30 minutes.
4 Meanwhile, heat the oven to 180C/350F/Gas 4.
5 Cut the dough into 36 equal pieces and shape into crescents (see Preparation), then transfer to 2 ungreased baking sheets.
6 Bake in the centre and just above centre of the oven for 12-15 minutes, until set and lightly coloured. Swap the sheets halfway through baking to ensure biscuits cook and colour evenly.
7 Cool the biscuits for 5 minutes, then loosen from the baking sheets, transfer to a wire rack and leave to cool completely. Sprinkle the biscuits with icing sugar.

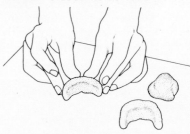

CHILDREN'S BISCUITS

BASIC BISCUIT DOUGH
500 g/1 lb plain flour
large pinch of salt
300 g/10 oz butter, diced
100 g/4 oz caster sugar
100 g/4 oz light soft brown sugar
2 eggs, lightly beaten
margarine, for greasing

1 Sift the flour and salt into a large bowl. Add the butter and rub into the flour until the mixture looks like fine breadcrumbs. Stir in the sugars, mixing well (see Variation).
2 Make a well in the centre, then stir in the eggs, to form a soft dough. Turn on to a lightly floured surface and knead gently until smooth. Divide the dough into quarters, wrap in cling film and refrigerate until needed.
3 Heat the oven to 180C/350F/Gas 4. Grease 4 large baking sheets.

Jammy owls

MAKES 12
¼ quantity basic biscuit dough
2-3 tablespoons seedless raspberry jam

1 Roll out the dough on a lightly floured surface to 5 mm/¼ inch thickness. Cut out 24 rounds with a 6 cm/2½ inch round fluted pastry cutter and place half the rounds on a greased baking sheet. Spread each one with raspberry jam almost to the edges.
2 Using a 2 cm/¾ inch plain cutter, cut out and discard 2 circles from the top half of the other rounds. Assemble biscuits (see Preparation).
3 Bake in oven for about 6 minutes. Cool owls on the baking sheet for 2 minutes, then transfer to a wire rack to cool completely.

Dominoes

MAKES 16
¼ quantity basic biscuit dough
1-2 tablespoons hazelnut spread
50 g/2 oz icing sugar
1½ teaspoons water

1 Roll out the dough on a lightly floured surface to a rectangle measuring 30 × 15 cm/12 × 6 inches. Cut dough in half lengthways, and then cut each half across into 8 strips.
2 Place on a greased baking sheet and bake in the oven for about 6 minutes. Cool on the baking sheet for 2 minutes. Transfer to a wire rack and leave the biscuits to cool completely.
3 Spread each biscuit with a little hazelnut spread. Sift the icing sugar into a small bowl and mix in the water. Place in a greaseproof icing bag and snip off the tip.
4 Pipe a straight line across the centre of each biscuit. Pipe several small dots in lines on both sides of centre line to represent 'dots' of a domino. Leave until icing is set.

Cotton tails

MAKES 8
¼ quantity basic biscuit dough
100 g/4 oz icing sugar
about 1 tablespoon orange juice
finely grated zest of 1 large orange
few drops of orange food colouring (optional)
4 white marshmallows, halved

1 Roll out the dough on a lightly floured surface to 5 mm/¼ inch thickness. Cut out 8 rabbit shapes with a 7.5 cm/3 inch long rabbit-shaped cutter. Transfer to a greased baking sheet.
2 Bake in oven for about 6 minutes

until golden brown. Cool on the baking sheet for 2 minutes, then transfer to a wire rack and leave to cool completely.
3 Sift the icing sugar into a bowl. Stir in just enough orange juice to give a thick coating consistency. Stir in the orange zest and, if liked, a few drops of orange food colouring.
4 Spread a little icing over each biscuit. Place a marshmallow half, cut side down on each biscuit to represent the tail. Leave to set.

Marzipan wheels

MAKES 20
¼ quantity basic biscuit dough
100 g/4 oz marzipan
few drops each of red and green food colouring
1 tablespoon apricot jam, warmed
½ teaspoon ground cinnamon
icing sugar, for dusting

1 Roll out the dough on a floured surface to a rectangle 30 × 20 cm/12 × 8 inches. Cut the rectangle in half across. Divide the marzipan in half. Knead red food colouring into one half, and the green into the other half.
2 Roll each piece of marzipan out on a surface dusted with icing sugar, to a rectangle measuring 20 × 15 cm/8 × 6 inches.
3 Brush one rectangle of dough lightly with jam and sprinkle with cinnamon. Top with a marzipan rectangle, brush again with jam and sprinkle over cinnamon. Continue layering with the remaining dough and the marzipan rectangles.
4 Starting at the shortest side, roll up the layers tightly. Wrap in greaseproof paper and refrigerate for 30 minutes. Cut into 20 rounds with a sharp knife, place on a greased baking sheet and bake for about 6 minutes.
5 Cool on the baking sheet for 3-4 minutes, [!] then transfer to a wire rack and allow to cool completely.

Cooks Notes

TIME

Making basic dough takes 15 minutes. Allow 20-30 minutes for making the different shapes plus chilling the wheels. Allow cooling time.

VARIATION

Add ¼ teaspoon ground spice to the basic biscuit dough.

- 290 calories/1225 kj per tail
- 95 calories/400 kj per domino
- 210 calories/875 kj per owl
- 90 calories/375 kj per wheel

PREPARATION

Assemble the jammy owls as follows:

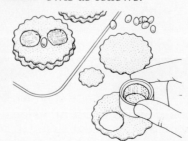

Place a cut-out round on top of each whole round. Press to seal, then make a nose from pastry trimmings.

WATCHPOINT
Cool the marzipan wheels on the baking sheet a few minutes longer than the other biscuits to prevent them cracking. However do not allow them to set on it. If this happens return them to the oven for a minute to soften.

FREEZING
Wrap dough in foil or in polythene bag. Seal, label and freeze up to 3 months. Defrost in the refrigerator for 1 hour until soft enough to roll.

Gingersnap clowns

MAKES 8

75 g/3 oz margarine
100 g/4 oz caster sugar

2 tablespoons golden syrup
175 g/6 oz plain flour
2 teaspoons ground ginger
½ teaspoon bicarbonate of soda
margarine, for greasing

ICING
50 g/2 oz icing sugar
about 2 teaspoons water

1 Heat the oven to 180C/350F/Gas 4 and grease 2 large baking sheets.
2 Put the margarine, sugar and syrup into a heavy-based saucepan and heat very gently, stirring, until melted. ⚠ Allow to cool slightly.
3 Meanwhile, sift the flour, ginger

Cook's Notes

TIME
30 minutes preparation, 10-12 minutes cooking, plus cooling and decorating.

WATCHPOINT
Keep the heat low and do not allow to boil or it will turn into toffee.

●180 calories/775 kj per clown

COOK'S TIPS
Use a gingerbread man biscuit cutter to cut out the clowns. If you do not have one, draw a clown shape on a piece of cardboard and cut out. Lay shape on rolled-out dough and cut round it with a knife.

Swap baking sheets halfway through cooking so that all the biscuits will brown evenly.

and bicarbonate of soda into a large bowl, then make a well in centre.
4 Add the melted mixture to the dry ingredients and mix with a wooden spoon to a firm dough.
5 Turn the dough out on to a lightly floured surface, divide into 8 and roll out each piece to 5 mm/¼ inch thickness, then cut each into a clown shape (see Cook's tips).
6 Using a fish slice, carefully lift the

biscuits on to the prepared baking sheets and bake for 10-12 minutes (see Cook's tips). Cool for 5 minutes then transfer to a wire rack. Leave until cold.
7 Meanwhile, make the icing: sift the icing sugar into a bowl and beat in the water. Spoon into a piping bag fitted with a plain writing nozzle.
8 Pipe a face and clothes on to the clowns and leave to set for 1 hour.

Chewy bars

MAKES 16
225 g/8 oz margarine or butter
200 g/7 oz porridge oats
50 g/2 oz flaked almonds
100 g/4 oz light soft brown sugar
75 g/3 oz desiccated coconut
margarine, for greasing

TO FINISH
100 g/4 oz plain dessert chocolate
(see Economy), broken into
pieces
25 g/1 oz flaked almonds

1 Heat the oven to 150C/300F/Gas 2. Grease a 30 × 20 cm/12 × 8 inch Swiss roll tin.
2 Put the margarine into a large, heavy-based pan and melt gently over very low heat, stirring occasionally. Remove from the heat, add the oats, almonds, sugar and coconut and mix together thoroughly.
3 Spoon the mixture into the prepared tin and press evenly over the base (see Cook's tip). Bake in the oven for 30-35 minutes, until set and golden brown. Cook for 5 minutes, then cut into 16 bars. Leave in the tin to cool completely.
4 Put the chocolate into a heatproof bowl over a pan of barely simmering water and leave until melted, stirring occasionally.
5 Meanwhile, transfer the bars to a wire rack and place a plate underneath. Remove the bowl from the water and spread the melted chocolate over the top of each bar. Sprinkle with flaked almonds ! and leave to set completely. Store in an airtight container.

Dolly daydreams

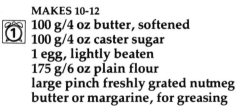

MAKES 10-12

100 g/4 oz butter, softened
100 g/4 oz caster sugar
1 egg, lightly beaten
175 g/6 oz plain flour
large pinch freshly grated nutmeg
butter or margarine, for greasing

TO FINISH
1-2 glacé cherries, cut into slivers
30-36 currants
chocolate dots or chips

1 Heat the oven to 180C/350F/Gas 4. Grease 2 large baking sheets.
2 Beat the butter and caster sugar together until pale and fluffy. Beat in the egg, a little at a time. Sift in the flour and nutmeg and mix to a firm dough.
3 Turn the dough out on to a lightly floured surface and knead briefly

until smooth. Roll out the dough to a thickness of about 5 mm/¼ inch, then cut into 10-12 dolly shaped biscuits (see Cook's tips).
4 Using a palette knife, carefully transfer the biscuits to the prepared baking sheets, spacing them slightly apart. Decorate with slivers of cherry for the lips, currants for the

eyes and nose and chocolate dots for buttons.
5 Bake in the oven for about 15 minutes (see Cook's tips), until the edges are lightly browned. Gently loosen each biscuit by sliding a palette knife underneath, then leave to cool for 10 minutes. Transfer to a wire rack to cool completely.

Cook's Notes

 TIME
25-30 minutes preparation, 15 minutes baking, plus cooling time.

 COOK'S TIPS
Some large stationers and hardware stores sell biscuit cutters in the shape of a lady or 'dolly'. If unavailable, draw your own dolly shape on a piece of stiff cardboard and cut this out. Lay the shape on the rolled out dough and carefully cut round it with a sharp knife.

Swap the baking sheets halfway through cooking.

 SERVING IDEAS
These biscuits are ideal for children's teas and birthday parties.

 VARIATION
Decorate each cold biscuit with piped glacé icing. Leave to set; serve within 2-3 hours

● 210 calories/880 kj per biscuit

Marzipan windmills

MAKES 9

75 g/3 oz almond marzipan
215 g/7½ oz frozen puff pastry, defrosted
15 g/½ oz butter

ICING
75 g/3 oz icing sugar
1 tablespoon water

TO DECORATE
thin strips of angelica
15 g/½ oz flaked almonds

1 Divide the marzipan into 9 equal-sized pieces. Roll into small balls and set aside.
2 Heat the oven to 220C/425F/Gas 7.
3 Roll out the pastry on a floured surface to a 30 cm/12 inch square. Using a sharp knife cut into 9 smaller squares, each about 10 cm/4 inches.
4 From each corner make a cut 5 cm/2 inches long, almost to the centre of each square so that you have 4 triangle shapes.
5 Take alternate points of the triangles to the centre of the pastry square to give a 'windmill' shape (see Preparation). Press down firmly. Complete the other squares in the same way and place on a dampened baking sheet.
6 Press a marzipan ball into the centre of each windmill, flattening it slightly. Refrigerate for 15 minutes.
7 Melt the butter in a small pan and brush over the pastries. Bake in the oven for 15-20 minutes until light brown. (The pastries colour quickly, so take care they do not burn.) Cool completely on a wire rack.
8 Sift the icing sugar into a bowl and mix in the water. Drizzle a little icing over each pastry and decorate with 3-4 angelica strips and a few almonds. Serve as soon as possible.

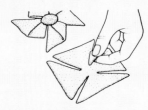

Tollhouse rockies

MAKES 12-14

225 g/8 oz plain flour
2 teaspoons baking powder
pinch of salt
100 g/4 oz margarine or butter
100 g/4 oz sugar
grated zest of 1 orange
75 g/3 oz plain chocolate drops
1 egg, lightly beaten
a little milk, to mix
melted fat or vegetable oil, for
    greasing

1 Heat the oven to 200C/400F/Gas 6. Lightly grease 2 baking sheets.
2 Sift the flour, baking powder and salt into a large bowl. Add the margarine and cut it into the flour with a knife, then rub in the pieces until the mixture resembles fine breadcrumbs.
3 Stir in the sugar, orange zest and chocolate drops. Using a fork, mix

in the egg, then stir in just enough milk to make a moist but stiff mixture. !
4 Using 2 forks, put the mixture on to the greased baking sheets in small rocky heaps (see Preparation). Make 12-14 heaps, spacing them well

apart to allow for spreading.
5 Bake the cakes in the oven for about 20 minutes until risen and browned. Lift the baked cakes on to a wire rack with a fish slice or palette knife and leave to cool. Serve fresh.

Cook's Notes

TIME
The cakes take about 20 minutes to prepare and 20 minutes to bake.

PREPARATION
Using 2 forks is the best way to achieve attractive rocky shapes:

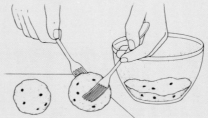
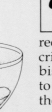

WATCHPOINT
Be careful how much milk you add—too much will cause the cakes to spread during baking as the mixture will be too slack to hold its shape well.

DID YOU KNOW
This is an adaptation of a traditional American recipe. Toll-house cookies (very crisp, small, melt-in-the-mouth biscuits) were originally offered to travellers paying their due at the toll gate.

●170 calories/700 kj per cake

Garibaldi biscuits

MAKES 24

100 g/4 oz self-raising flour
pinch of salt
25 g/1 oz caster sugar
40 g/1½ oz margarine or butter,
  diced
about 3 tablespoons milk
50 g/2 oz currants
beaten egg, to glaze
margarine or butter, for greasing

1 Heat the oven to 200C/400F/Gas 6. Grease a large baking sheet.

2 Sift the flour and salt into a bowl, then stir in the sugar. Add the margarine and rub it in with your fingertips until the mixture resembles fine breadcrumbs. Add 2 tablespoons milk and mix to a fairly firm dough.

3 Turn the dough out on to a lightly floured surface and knead briefly until smooth, then roll out to a 23 cm/9 inch square.

4 Cut the dough in half with a sharp knife. Brush one half generously with milk and sprinkle evenly with the currants. Place the remaining piece of dough on top and press down lightly. !

5 Roll out to a rectangle, about 25 × 20 cm/10 × 8 inches. Trim the edges with a sharp knife, then cut into 24 fingers. Brush the tops generously with beaten egg.

6 Using a palette knife, place the biscuits, just touching, on the prepared baking sheet. Bake in the oven, just above the centre, for 10-12 minutes, until browned. !

7 Let the biscuits 'settle' for a few seconds, then transfer to a wire rack and leave to cool completely. Break apart to serve.

Cook's Notes

TIME
Preparation and baking take about 45 minutes. Cooling takes about 15 minutes.

WATCHPOINTS
The milk makes the work surface sticky, so clean and flour it again.

Keep an eye on the time and use the oven timer if you have one, as it is very easy to over-bake these biscuits.

DID YOU KNOW
These biscuits are named after the famous Italian general Garibaldi, who was reputed to be extremely partial to them.

STORAGE
The biscuits will keep for up to 1 week in an airtight container.

●40 calories/150 kj per biscuit

Macaroons

MAKES 18

175 g/6 oz ground almonds
175 g/6 oz caster sugar

few drops of almond flavouring
few drops of vanilla flavouring
2 small egg whites, lightly beaten
blanched almonds, to decorate
extra caster sugar, for sprinkling

1 Heat the oven to 180C/350F/Gas 4. Line 2 large baking sheets with rice paper.
2 Put the ground almonds and caster sugar into a bowl and mix together well with a wooden spoon. Add the flavourings, then gradually stir in just enough egg white to give a fairly stiff consistency. !
3 Put the mixture into a piping bag fitted with a 1 cm/½ inch plain nozzle (see Cook's tip). Pipe nine 4 cm/1½ inch rounds on to each prepared baking sheet. Space rounds well apart, and away from the edges of the baking sheets, to allow room for spreading.
4 Place 1 almond in centre of each round; sprinkle lightly with caster sugar. Bake in the oven for 10-15 minutes, until just firm and beginning to colour.
5 Cool the biscuits for 1-2 minutes, then transfer to wire racks and leave to cool completely. Using your fingers, flake the excess rice paper off the biscuits. Serve at once, or store in a tin or other airtight container for up to 5 days.

Cook's Notes

TIME
The biscuits take less than 1 hour to prepare, bake and cool.

 WATCHPOINT
The mixture should be just firm enough to hold its shape. If it is too runny it will spread and flatten badly during baking.

 COOK'S TIP
If you do not want to pipe, put heaped table-spoons of the mixture on to the baking sheets.

● 100 calories/425 kj per biscuit

Fruit and nut crispies

MAKES 18

50 g/2 oz plain flour
50 g/2 oz porridge oats
25 g/1 oz butter
100 g/4 oz stoned dates,
   chopped (see Cook's tip)
25 g/1 oz shelled walnuts,
   chopped
25 g/1 oz fresh peanuts, skinned
   and chopped
25 g/1 oz cut mixed peel,
   chopped
½ teaspoon freshly grated nutmeg
½ teaspoon ground cinnamon
75 g/3 oz light soft brown sugar
2-3 tablespoons cold water
25 g/1 oz glacé cherries, chopped, to
   decorate
vegetable oil, for greasing

1 Brush a baking sheet with oil. Heat the oven to 200C/400F/Gas 6.
2 Sift the flour into a bowl and add the oats. Add the butter and rub it in with your fingertips. Mix in the dates, nuts, peel, spices and sugar. Add just enough cold water to make a firm dough.
3 Using a teaspoon, divide the dough into 18 small balls and shape them into flattened rounds about 5 cm/2 inches across (see Preparation). Place on the baking sheet and press a piece of cherry in the middle of each round.
4 Bake in the oven for 8-10 minutes until golden. Cool on a wire rack.

Cook's Notes

TIME
The biscuits take about 40 minutes to make.

WATCHPOINT
Add water very gradually so that the dough does not become too sticky to handle.

COOK'S TIP
For speed, put the dates, walnuts, peanuts and peel through a mincer instead of chopping them.

VARIATION
Try using dried prunes, figs or apricots in place of the chopped dates.

PREPARATION
To shape the teaspoonfuls of dough into rounds:

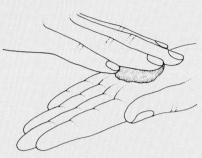

Use your hands to form the mixture into balls, then flatten gently with your fingers.

● 85 calories/355 kj per biscuit

Savoury sage biscuits

MAKES 36

175 g/6 oz plain flour
75 g/3 oz semolina
1 teaspoon salt
175 g/6 oz butter, at room
    temperature, diced
100 g/4 oz mature Cheddar cheese,
    finely grated
vegetable oil, for greasing

FILLING
200 g/7 oz full-fat soft cheese
1 teaspoon finely chopped fresh
    sage, or ½ teaspoon dried sage

1 Heat the oven to 180C/350F/Gas 4.
Lightly grease 2 baking sheets.
2 Sift the flour with the semolina
and salt into a large bowl. Add the
butter and rub it in with your
fingertips then stir in the cheese.

3 Draw the mixture together and
knead briefly in the bowl to make a
firm dough. Turn out on to a lightly
floured surface and roll out to a
thickness of 5 mm/¼ inch.
4 Using 2.5 cm/1 inch petits fours
cutters, cut the dough into as many
biscuits as possible (see Cook's tip).
Knead the trimmings together, roll
out again and cut out more biscuits.
You should make 72.
5 Transfer the biscuits to the prepared baking sheets, spacing them
slightly apart to allow for spread-

ing. Bake in centre and just below
centre of the oven for 20-25 minutes, swapping the baking sheets
after 10 minutes cooking time. [!]
6 Cool the biscuits for a few minutes, then transfer to wire racks
and leave for about 30 minutes to
cool completely (see Storage).
7 Make the filling: beat the cheese
until very soft and creamy, then
beat in the sage until it is evenly
incorporated.
8 Sandwich the biscuits in pairs
with the sage filling. Serve as soon
as possible, while still crisp.

Cook's Notes

TIME
20 minutes preparation,
plus baking and cooling
for the biscuits. Allow about 10
minutes for sandwiching the
biscuits with the filling.

COOK'S TIP
Use a variety of cutters,
but be sure to cut an
even number of each shape or
you will not be able to sandwich
the biscuits together.

WATCHPOINT
Keep an eye on the bis-
cuits as they brown
quickly and can easily burn.
The biscuits will spread if the
oven temperature is too high.

STORAGE
The biscuits can be
stored, unfilled, in an
airtight container for 1 week.

●90 calories/375 kj per pair

Curry biscuits

MAKES 30

2 teaspoons hot curry powder
100 g/4 oz plain flour
salt and freshly ground black pepper
100 g/4 oz margarine or butter,
  diced
50 g/2 oz Cheddar cheese, finely
  grated
2 egg yolks, beaten
1 tablespoon finely chopped
  peanuts
1 tablespoon Bombay Mix (see
  Buying guide)
2 teaspoons sesame seeds

1 Heat the oven to 190C/375F/Gas 5.
Grease 2 baking sheets.
2 Sift the flour and curry powder
into a bowl with salt and pepper to
taste. Add the margarine and rub it
in until the mixture resembles fine
breadcrumbs. Stir in the cheese,
then add three-quarters of the egg
yolks and mix to a stiff dough.
3 Roll out the dough on a lightly
floured board until 5 mm/¼ inch
thick. Cut the dough into about
30 rounds with a 5 cm/2 inch fluted
biscuit cutter.
4 Transfer the curry biscuits to the
greased baking sheets, spacing them
apart, then brush lightly with the
remaining egg yolk. Sprinkle the
peanuts on one-third of the biscuits,
the Bombay Mix on another third
and the sesame seeds on the rest.
Bake in the centre and just below
centre of the oven for 20 minutes,
swapping baking sheets after 10
minutes cooking.
5 Leave on sheets for 2 minutes to
firm up, then carefully transfer to a
wire rack to cool completely before
serving (see Storage).

Cook's Notes

 TIME
Preparation takes about
25 minutes plus about
20 minutes baking.

 STORAGE
The biscuits will keep
fresh and crisp in an
airtight container for 4 days.

 BUYING GUIDE
Bombay Mix is some-
times sold as Bombay
Crunch and is widely available
in health food shops, Indian
shops, delicatessens and some
street markets. It is a spicy
mixture of cooked dried
noodles, nuts and pulses.

SERVING IDEAS
These savoury biscuits
make a good base for
canapés to serve with drinks –
top with cream cheese and
prawns or hard-boiled egg; dust
with cayenne or chives.

● 50 calories/225 kj per biscuit

Date rolls

MAKES 18
250 g/9 oz self-raising flour
175 g/6 oz margarine, diced
25 g/1 oz caster sugar
1 egg, beaten
melted fat or vegetable oil, for greasing

FILLING AND GLAZE
250 g/9 oz stoned dates (see Buying guide), chopped
finely grated zest and juice of 1 large orange
2 trifle sponge cakes, crumbled
1 tablespoon milk
2 tablespoons caster sugar

1 Sift the flour into a bowl. Rub in the margarine, then stir in the sugar. Add 2 tablespoons of the beaten egg and mix to a stiff dough.
2 Turn the dough out on to a lightly floured surface and knead briefly until smooth. Wrap in cling film and refrigerate.
3 To make the filling: mix the dates, orange zest and juice together in a saucepan. Cover and cook over very low heat for about 10 minutes, until the dates are soft. Remove from the heat and stir in the crumbled sponges. Set aside to cool completely.
4 Heat the oven to 190C/375F/Gas 5. Grease a large baking sheet.
5 Cut the dough into 3 equal pieces. On a lightly floured surface, roll out each piece to a 30 × 10 cm/12 × 4 inch rectangle. Trim the edges.
6 Divide the date mixture into 3. With your hands, shape each into a roll, 30 cm/12 inches long. Place a date roll lengthways on each rectangle of dough, close to the edge, then roll up from a long edge, to enclose the date filling.

7 Beat the milk with the remaining egg and brush over the rolls, then sprinkle with caster sugar. Cut each roll across into 6 pieces and transfer to the prepared baking sheet.
8 Bake in the oven for 20-25 minutes until golden. Loosen the rolls with a palette knife; cool on a wire rack.

Cook's Notes

TIME
1½ hours preparation, 20-25 minutes baking, plus cooling time.

BUYING GUIDE
Ready-stoned dates are sold either pressed into blocks, or loose in bags. Do not use the sugar-coated kind; they are too sweet for this recipe.

●205 calories/850 kj per roll

Muesli munchies

350 g/12 oz muesli
(see Cook's tips)
6 tablespoons sunflower or
vegetable oil
4 tablespoons clear honey
4 tablespoons golden syrup
½ teaspoon vanilla flavouring
extra oil, for greasing

1 Heat the oven to 180C/350F/Gas 4. Thoroughly grease two 16 cm/ 6½ inch round sandwich tins, then line the base of each tin with a round of non-stick vegetable parchment paper.

2 Place the muesli in a large bowl. Add the oil, honey, syrup and vanilla and stir until well mixed. Spoon half the mixture into each tin, press evenly over the base, then Level each surface with the back of a large metal spoon. (Dip spoon into hot water to prevent sticking.)

3 Bake in the oven for about 15 minutes, or until golden brown (see Cook's tips). Cool the rounds for 5 minutes, then cut each round into 6 wedges with a small, sharp knife. ⚠

4 Using a round-bladed knife, loosen the wedges from the sides of the tin. Leave to cool completely, then remove from the tins (see Serving ideas and Storage).

Cook's Notes

TIME
10 minutes preparation, plus about 15 minutes baking and 1 hour to cool.

WATCHPOINT
Be sure to cut right through the mixture, or the wedges will stick together.

COOK'S TIPS
Use any brand of muesli cereal available, but if it contains large pieces of fruit or nuts chop them before using or the rounds will be difficult to cut.

The mixture is very soft when the tins are removed from the oven; it firms up as it cools.

SERVING IDEAS
These wedges make a wholesome and nutritious addition to packed lunches and picnic hampers.

STORAGE
The wedges will stay fresh and chewy for 2-3 weeks in an airtight container.

●205 calories/875 kj per wedge

Custard creams

MAKES 14

50 g/2 oz self-raising flour
50 g/2 oz custard powder (see Did
  you know)
50 g/2 oz butter or margarine,
  softened
50 g/2 oz caster sugar
1 egg yolk, lightly beaten
vegetable oil, for greasing

FILLING

15 g/½ oz butter or margarine,
  softened
25 g/1 oz icing sugar, sifted
2 teaspoons lemon juice

1 Heat the oven to 170C/325F/Gas 3.
Grease 2 baking sheets or trays.
2 Sift the flour and custard powder
into a bowl. In a separate large bowl,
beat the butter and caster sugar
together until pale and fluffy. Beat
in the egg, a little at a time, then
gradually work in the flour mixture
to make a firm dough.
3 Turn the dough out on to a lightly
floured surface and knead briefly,
then roll it out to a 25 cm/10 inch
circle. Using a plain or fluted 4 cm/
1½ inch round cutter, cut the dough
into as many rounds as possible.
Knead the trimmings together, roll
out again and cut into more rounds
until there are 28 altogether.
4 Place the rounds on the prepared
baking sheets and prick well with a
fork. Bake on centre shelf and just
above for 20-25 minutes, until
lightly browned (see Cook's tip).
Cool the biscuits for a few seconds,
then loosen them with a palette
knife and transfer to a wire rack.
Leave to cool completely.
5 Meanwhile, make the filling: beat
the butter until very soft and
creamy, then gradually beat in the
icing sugar. Add the lemon juice, 1
teaspoon at a time, and beat well
until smoothly blended.
6 Sandwich the biscuits in pairs
with the creamy filling and serve
them as soon as possible.

Moist treacle bars

MAKES 10-12

50 g/2 oz margarine
50 g/2 oz dark soft brown sugar
125 ml/4 fl oz black treacle
2 tablespoons natural yoghurt
1 large egg, lightly beaten
100 g/4 oz plain flour
¼ teaspoon bicarbonate of soda
1½ teaspoons ground mixed spice
1 tablespoon ground allspice
1 tablespoon ground cinnamon
vegetable oil, for greasing

1 Heat the oven to 170C/325F/Gas 3. Thoroughly grease a shallow 25 × 15 cm/10 × 6 inch baking tin.
2 Put the margarine into a heavy-based saucepan with the sugar and treacle. Heat gently, stirring often, until the margarine has melted and the brown sugar has dissolved. Remove from the heat and cool for

5 minutes, then add yoghurt and egg and beat with a wooden spoon until well blended.
3 Sift the flour into a large bowl with the soda and spices. Make a well in the centre. Pour the treacle mixture into the well, then stir until evenly blended. [!]
4 Turn mixture into prepared

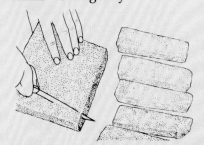
tin and then level the surface. Bake in the oven for 35-40 minutes, until risen and springy to the touch, then leave the cake in the tin until it is completely cool.
5 Lift out of the tin, cut cake into bars (see Preparation) and store in an airtight container for at least 2 days before serving.

Oaty crisps

MAKES 28-30
175 g/6 oz porridge oats
100 g/4 oz soft brown sugar (see Cook's tip)
125 ml/4 fl oz corn or sunflower oil
1 egg, lightly beaten
½ teaspoon vanilla flavouring
extra oil, for greasing

1 Heat the oven to 170C/325F/Gas 3. Brush 2 baking sheets with oil.
2 Place the oats, sugar and oil in a large bowl and mix thoroughly together with a wooden spoon. Add the egg and vanilla and stir vigorously until evenly mixed.
3 Using a teaspoon, put 28-30 equal-sized heaps of the mixture on to the prepared baking sheet, spacing them well apart. Flatten into rounds (see Preparation), then bake

in the oven for 15-20 minutes, until they set and are golden brown.
4 Cool the biscuits for 1 minute, then loosen with a palette knife,

transfer to wire racks and leave to cool completely. Serve as soon as possible, or store in an airtight container (see Storage).

Cook's Notes

TIME
Preparation time (including baking) is about 30 minutes. Cooling takes about 1 hour.

COOK'S TIP
Use either light or dark soft brown sugar. (Dark sugar gives a stronger caramel flavour and deeper colour.) Sift the sugar, pressing it through the sieve, if it is lumpy.

STORAGE
Store the biscuits as soon as they are cold. They will stay crisp and crunchy for up to 1 week.

PREPARATION
Shape the biscuits as follows:

Using a dampened palette knife, flatten each heap of mixture. (Rinse blade in cold water when mixture sticks to it.) Neaten edges with side of the knife.

● 75 calories/325 kj per biscuit

Chewy nut cookies

MAKES 24

100 g/4 oz pecan nuts, chopped
100 g/4 oz butter, softened
75 g/3 oz cream cheese
½ teaspoon vanilla flavouring
175 g/6 oz caster sugar
225 g/8 oz plain flour
½ teaspoon salt

Cook's Notes

TIME
Preparation takes about 15 minutes. Baking in the oven takes 12 minutes. Allow a further 30-40 minutes cooling time.

COOK'S TIPS
For a decorative finish, use a tumbler with a pebbled base to press out the cookies. If a plain tumbler is used, make a criss-cross pattern on the cookies with a fork before baking.

At the end of baking time the cookies will look quite pale and they should be quite soft. They firm up during cooling, but will still have a chewy texture.

● 130 calories/525 kj per portion

1 Heat the oven to 190C/375F/Gas 5.
2 Using a wooden spoon, beat the butter with the cheese in a mixing bowl until light and creamy. Beat in the vanilla flavouring, then gradually beat in the sugar.
3 Sift the flour with the salt and gradually beat into the mixture. Stir in the chopped pecan nuts with a fork until evenly distributed through the mixture.
4 Roll the dough into balls about 2.5 cm/1 inch in diameter. Place the balls about 5 cm/2 inches apart on ungreased baking sheets. Using the base of a tumbler dipped in water, press the balls of dough out into 5 cm/2 inch rounds (see Cook's tips).
5 Bake in the oven for 12 minutes (see Cook's tips). Remove from oven and leave to cool on the sheets for 2-3 minutes. Transfer the cookies with a fish slice to wire racks and leave to cool completely.

Parkin biscuits

MAKES 12

50 g/2 oz plain flour
½ teaspoon bicarbonate of soda
¼ teaspoon ground ginger
¼ teaspoon ground cinnamon
50 g/2 oz medium oatmeal
50 g/2 oz margarine, diced
40 g/1½ oz sugar
1 tablespoon golden syrup
15-25 g/½-1 oz cut mixed peel, to
    finish (optional)
margarine, for greasing

1 Heat the oven to 180C/350F/Gas 4.
Grease a large baking sheet.

2 Sift the flour, bicarbonate of soda and spices into a bowl, then stir in the oatmeal. Add the margarine and rub it in with your fingertips until the mixture resembles fine bread-crumbs. Stir in the sugar and syrup, then gather together to a soft dough.

3 Divide the dough into 12 equal pieces. Using your hands, roll each piece into a ball, then place well apart on the prepared baking sheet. Put a little cut peel on the top of each one if liked, then flatten slightly with the back of a fork.

4 Bake in the oven for 10-15 minutes, until set and light golden in colour. Cool the biscuits for 5 minutes, then loosen from the baking sheet with a palette knife and transfer to a wire rack. Leave to cool completely. !

Cook's Notes

TIME
30-35 minutes prepara-
tion (including baking),
plus cooling time.

WATCHPOINTS
Handle the biscuits carefully as they are fragile while warm, and liable to break.

If not serving the biscuits at once, store them in an airtight container otherwise they will soften. They can be stored for up to 5 days, preferably in a cool, dry place.

●95 calories/405 kj per biscuit

Coconut bars

MAKES 10
75 g/3 oz self-raising flour
½ teaspoon baking powder
50 g/2 oz butter, at room
   temperature (see Watchpoint)
50 g/2 oz caster sugar
2 tablespoons milk
1 egg
extra butter, for greasing

COCONUT TOPPING
1 egg white
50 g/2 oz Demerara sugar
50 g/2 oz desiccated coconut

1 Heat the oven to 180C/350F/Gas 4. Grease a shallow 18 cm/7 inch square cake tin, line base with greaseproof paper, then grease the paper.
2 Sift the flour and baking powder into a large bowl. Add the butter, caster sugar, milk and egg and beat together with a wooden spoon for 2-3 minutes, until evenly blended.
3 Turn the cake mixture into the prepared tin and level the surface.
4 Make the topping: in a clean, dry bowl, whisk the egg white until standing in stiff peaks. Using a large metal spoon, lightly fold the Demerara sugar and coconut into the whisked egg white.
5 Spoon the coconut topping on to the cake mixture, then spread it thinly over the top with the back of a fork. Bake in the oven for 25-30 minutes, until the topping is crisp, golden brown and firm to the touch.
6 Cool the cake for 2-3 minutes, then run a palette knife around the sides to loosen it and carefully turn out on to a wire rack. Peel off the lining paper, then turn the cake topping side up and leave for about 1 hour to cool completely.
7 To serve: cut cake in half, then cut each half across into 5 bars.

Spiced thins

MAKES 20-25

 225 g/8 oz plain flour
1½ teaspoons ground ginger
 1½ teaspoons ground cinnamon
100 g/4 oz margarine or butter,
   diced
175 g/6 oz light soft brown sugar,
   sifted (see Watchpoints)
1 large egg, lightly beaten
icing sugar, for dusting (optional)
vegetable oil, for greasing

1 Sift the flour and spices into a bowl. Rub in the margarine until the mixture resembles fine crumbs, then stir in the sugar. Using a round-bladed knife, mix in the egg.
2 Gather the mixture together with your fingers to make a soft dough, turn out on to a lightly floured surface and knead briefly until smooth. Shape into a short roll, 7.5 cm/3 inches in diameter, then wrap it in cling film, place on a plate and refrigerate for at least 2 hours to firm.

3 Heat the oven to 190C/375F/Gas 5. Lightly oil 2 baking sheets.
4 Unwrap the roll (see Cook's tips) and cut off 5-6 wafer thin slices with a very sharp knife. Place the slices on 1 prepared baking sheet, spacing about 4 cm/1½ inches apart to allow for the mixture spreading during cooking.
5 Bake in the oven for about 12 minutes, until the edges are lightly browned. Meanwhile, cut another 5-6 thin slices from the roll (see

Cook's tips) and arrange on the other prepared baking sheet.
6 Remove the cooked biscuits from the oven and, using a palette knife, immediately transfer them to a wire rack to cool and crisp. Bake the second batch of biscuits in the same way as the first. Continue making biscuits, re-greasing the baking sheets as necessary, until all the dough is used.
7 Dust the biscuits with icing sugar, if liked, just before serving.

Cook's Notes

 TIME
The preparation takes 10 minutes plus chilling time for the dough; shaping and baking the biscuits takes about 1 hour. You will need to allow extra time for cooling.

WATCHPOINTS
It is essential to sift the sugar as any lumps will spoil the biscuits.
   Make sure there are no holes in the roll of dough or the look of the biscuits will be spoilt.

COOK'S TIPS
If the roll has flattened, gently reshape it so the slices will be round.
   If dough softens, return it to the refrigerator until it has firmed up again.

 STORAGE
The biscuits will stay crisp for up to 1 week when stored in an airtight container.

●105 calories/450 kj per biscuit

Cinnamon stars

MAKES ABOUT 35
75 g/3 oz plain flour
2 teaspoons ground cinnamon
100 g/4 oz ground almonds
2 small egg whites
75 g/3 oz caster sugar
¼ teaspoon almond flavouring
caster sugar, for dredging
lightly beaten egg white, to glaze
vegetable oil, for greasing

1 Sift the flour and cinnamon into a bowl, then stir in the almonds.
2 In a clean, dry bowl, whisk the egg whites until standing in stiff peaks. Whisk in the caster sugar, a little at a time.
3 Using a large metal spoon, stir in the flavouring, then gently fold in the flour mixture to make a soft, sticky dough. Refrigerate for 30 minutes to firm slightly.
4 Sprinkle the work surface generously with caster sugar. Place the dough on the sugar and lay a sheet of greaseproof paper over it (see Cook's tip). Roll out the dough to a thickness of 5 mm/¼ inch.

Carefully peel off greaseproof paper.
5 Heat the oven to 150C/300F/Gas 2. Lightly grease 2 baking trays or baking sheets.
6 Using a small (petits fours) star-shaped cutter, cut the dough into as many biscuits as possible. Gather the trimmings together, roll out in the same way as before and cut into more biscuits. You should make about 35.
7 Using a palette knife, transfer some of the biscuits to the prepared baking sheets, spacing them well apart. Brush with egg white, then bake in the oven for 10-15 minutes or until brown and just firm to the touch.
8 Leave the cooked biscuits for a few seconds, then loosen with a palette knife, place on a wire rack and sprinkle with caster sugar. Cool completely (see Storage).
9 Re-grease the baking sheets and glaze, bake and cool the remaining biscuits in the same way.

Chocolate kisses

MAKES ABOUT 15

175 g/6 oz margarine or butter,
  softened
50 g/2 oz icing sugar
175 g/6 oz plain flour
25 g/1 oz cocoa powder
vegetable oil, for greasing
icing sugar, to finish

ORANGE FILLING
50 g/2 oz margarine or butter,
  softened
100 g/4 oz icing sugar
grated zest of 1 orange
1 teaspoon orange juice

1 Heat the oven to 190C/375F/Gas 5.
Grease a large baking sheet.
2 Beat the margarine and icing
sugar together until pale and fluffy.
Sift the flour and cocoa powder into
a separate bowl. Using a hand-held
electric whisk or a wooden spoon,
gradually work the flour mixture
into the fluffy sugar mixture to make
a soft, sticky dough.
3 Put the dough into a piping bag
filled with a large star nozzle and
pipe about 30 small rosettes on to
the baking sheet (see Preparation).
4 Bake the biscuits in the oven for
15 minutes, or until firm underneath. ⚠ Cool the biscuits on the
baking sheet for 5 minutes, then use
a palette knife to transfer them to a
wire rack. Leave to cool completely.
5 Meanwhile, make the filling: beat
the margarine and icing sugar
together until pale and fluffy, then
beat in the orange zest and juice.
6 Sandwich kisses in pairs with
filling. Sift over icing sugar and
serve within 1-2 hours.

Cook's Notes

TIME
30 minutes preparation,
plus 15 minutes baking
and 30 minutes cooling.

WATCHPOINT
Check that the under-
sides of the biscuits are
firm and set before removing
from the oven, otherwise they
will crumble.

STORAGE
The unfilled biscuits
can be stored in an air-
tight container for 1 week.

● 210 calories/875 kj each

PREPARATION
Put the dough into a
piping bag and pipe it
on to the prepared baking sheet.

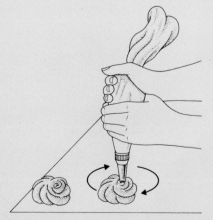

1 To pipe a rosette, hold the bag
upright and close to the surface of
the baking sheet.

2 Exerting gentle pressure, move
nozzle in a tight, complete circle.
Lift nozzle sharply.

Coconut shorties

MAKES 27

100 g/4 oz margarine, softened
100 g/4 oz caster sugar

100 g/4 oz plain flour, sifted
100 g/4 oz desiccated coconut
1 tablespoon milk
extra caster sugar (optional)
vegetable oil, for greasing

1 Heat the oven to 180C/350F/Gas 4. Grease 2 large baking sheets.
2 Beat the margarine and caster sugar together until pale and fluffy. Using a fork, gradually work in the flour and coconut. Stir in the milk, then gather the mixture together with your fingers to make a soft but not too sticky dough.
3 Turn the dough out on to a lightly floured surface and knead very briefly until smooth, then wrap and refrigerate for 10-15 minutes.

4 Roll out the dough on a lightly floured surface to a 23 cm/9 inch square. [!] Trim the edges with a sharp knife, then cut the square into 3 strips, each 23 × 7.5 cm/9 × 3 inches. [!] Cut each strip into 9 'fingers', each 2.5 cm/1 inch wide.
5 Using a palette knife, carefully transfer the biscuits to the prepared baking sheets, spacing them 2.5 cm/1 inch apart to allow for spreading. Bake the biscuits in the oven [!] for about 15 minutes, until tinged with brown.
6 Allow the biscuits to 'settle' for 1-2 minutes, then ease off the baking sheets and transfer to a wire rack with a palette knife. Leave to cool completely. Just before serving, dust with caster sugar, if liked.

Cook's Notes

TIME
35 minutes (including baking). Cooling takes about 15 minutes.

WATCHPOINTS
Use a lightly floured rolling pin as this soft dough is prone to stick.
Cut cleanly, without dragging the dough, otherwise the baked biscuits will be ragged.
Swap the position of the sheets halfway through baking time.

VARIATION
Blend 200 g/7 oz sifted icing sugar with just enough water to give a thick coating consistency, then tint pink with food colouring if liked. Spread the icing over each biscuit, sprinkle with shredded (sweetened and tenderized) long-strand coconut and leave to set. If possible serve the biscuits on the day of icing.

● 80 calories/325 kj per biscuit

Crunchy ginger biscuits

MAKES ABOUT 30

225 g/8 oz wholemeal flour (see Buying guide)
1½ teaspoons ground ginger
1 teaspoon bicarbonate of soda
100 g/4 oz margarine, softened
100 g/4 oz Demerara sugar
1 egg, lightly beaten
1 tablespoon clear honey
25 g/1 oz desiccated coconut
25 g/1 oz fine oatmeal
margarine, for greasing

1 Heat the oven to 180C/350F/Gas 4. Lightly grease 2 baking sheets.
2 Sift the flour with the ginger and bicarbonate of soda and reserve.
3 In a large bowl, beat margarine and the sugar together until light and fluffy. Add the egg, a little at a time, beating vigorously after each

addition. [!] Beat in the honey. With a large metal spoon, gradually fold in the flour, followed by the coconut and oatmeal.
4 Divide the mixture into 30 equal pieces and shape each into a round between the palms of your hands. Place rounds on prepared baking

sheets and space them well apart.
5 Mark each biscuit with the prongs of a fork, then bake in the oven for 10-15 minutes, until golden brown.
6 Allow the biscuits to 'settle' for about 1 minute. [!] Transfer to a wire rack and leave to cool completely (see Storage).

Cook's Notes

TIME
20-30 minutes preparation (including baking), plus 50-60 minutes to cool.

BUYING GUIDE
Good supermarkets and health food stores stock the plain wholemeal flour needed for this recipe. Do not use strong wholemeal flour (for bread-making) as this will produce tough biscuits.

● 75 calories/325 kj per biscuit

STORAGE
Store the biscuits in an airtight container as soon as they are cold. They will keep for up to 2 weeks.

WATCHPOINTS
Add the egg slowly to avoid the margarine and sugar mixture curdling.
The biscuits need to firm slightly: if removed from the sheets while still very hot and soft they could lose their attractive round shape.

Tiger biscuits

MAKES 15-20

175 g/6 oz margarine or butter
100 g/4 oz caster sugar
1 large egg, beaten
few drops of vanilla essence
175 g/6 oz plain flour, sifted
50 g/2 oz cornflour, sifted
melted margarine, for greasing

ICING

50 g/2 oz margarine or butter
175 g/6 oz icing sugar, sifted
2 teaspoons instant coffee powder
1 tablespoon hot milk

TO FINISH

75 g/3 oz chocolate vermicelli
15 g/½ oz icing sugar

1 Heat the oven to 190C/375F/Gas 5. Brush 3 baking sheets with melted margarine (see Cook's tips).
2 Put the margarine and sugar into a bowl and beat together with a wooden spoon until light and fluffy. Beat in the egg and vanilla essence, then use a metal spoon to fold in the flour and cornflour. Bind the mixture together with one hand to form a stiff ball of dough.
3 Transfer the dough to a well-floured board. Using a floured rolling pin, roll out the dough to about 2 mm/⅛ inch thick. Cut into rounds with a lightly floured 5 cm/2 inch diameter plain or fluted biscuit cutter. Transfer carefully to the baking sheets, placing them well apart. Lightly bind the trimmings together, roll and shape them until the dough has all been used.
4 Bake each sheet of biscuit dough in the oven for 10-15 minutes, until set and barely coloured. Leave on the sheets for 1-2 minutes, then transfer to wire racks with a fish slice and set aside until cool.
5 Meanwhile, make the icing: put the margarine into a bowl and beat until soft, then beat in the icing sugar. Dissolve the coffee powder in the milk and beat into the icing.
6 Sandwich the cooled biscuits together in pairs with a layer of icing, then spread a little icing around the sides.
7 Sprinkle the chocolate vermicelli over a plate and roll the biscuits in it to coat the sides. Sift icing sugar lightly over the tops of the biscuits.

Cook's Notes

TIME
The biscuit dough takes 20 minutes to prepare and a total of 30 minutes to cook. Allow at least another 45 minutes to cool, sandwich and decorate.

COOK'S TIPS
If you have only 1 or 2 baking sheets, wash up and regrease them before cooking another batch of biscuits.
Put the first sheet of biscuits in the oven as soon as they have been cut out, then carry on cutting out while they are cooking.

FREEZING
Open freeze until firm, then pack in rigid containers, seal, label and freeze for up to 3 months. To serve: defrost the biscuits unwrapped at room temperature for 3-4 hours, then decorate.

●220 calories/925 kj per biscuit

Brown sugar cinnamon cookies

MAKES 16

175 g/6 oz dark soft brown sugar
¾ teaspoon ground cinnamon
100 g/4 oz margarine, softened
1 teaspoon vanilla flavouring
150 g/5 oz plain flour
¼ teaspoon salt
vegetable oil, for greasing

1 Heat the oven to 190C/375F/Gas 5. Grease 2 baking sheets.
2 Grind the sugar, in batches, to a fine powder in an electric grinder or use a food processor. Mix 50 g/2 oz sugar with ¼ teaspoon cinnamon, then spread over a flat plate and reserve for the coating.
3 Put the remaining sugar into a large bowl with the margarine and beat together until pale and fluffy.

Then beat in the vanilla flavouring.
4 Sift the flour with the salt and remaining cinnamon, then add to the margarine and sugar mixture. Beat with a wooden spoon until the mixture begins to cling together, then work to a soft, slightly sticky dough with your hands.
5 Divide the dough into 16 equal pieces. Roll each piece into a ball between the palms of your hands and place on the prepared baking sheets, spacing them well apart to allow for spreading of the dough.
6 Bake the biscuits in the oven for about 20 minutes, or until set and just beginning to brown.
7 Using a palette knife, lift 1 biscuit off a baking sheet and place in the reserved sugar mixture on the plate. Turn the biscuit over, so that both sides are coated, then transfer to a wire rack. Coat the rest of the biscuits in sugar mixture in the same way and leave to cool completely before serving (see Storage).

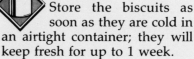

 TIME
15 minutes preparation and 20 minutes baking.

STORAGE
Store the biscuits as soon as they are cold in an airtight container; they will keep fresh for up to 1 week.

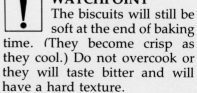 **WATCHPOINT**
The biscuits will still be soft at the end of baking time. (They become crisp as they cool.) Do not overcook or they will taste bitter and will have a hard texture.

●120 calories/500 kj per biscuit

Coconut crisps

MAKES 28

100 g/4 oz self-raising flour
pinch of salt
1 teaspoon ground cinnamon
100 g/4 oz caster sugar
100 g/4 oz soft tub margarine
1 egg
75 g/3 oz desiccated coconut
vegetable oil, for greasing

1 Heat the oven to 180C/350F/Gas 4. Grease 2 large baking sheets.

2 Sift the flour, salt and cinnamon into a bowl. Add the caster sugar, margarine and egg. Mix with a wooden spoon until evenly blended, then beat for 1-2 minutes. Mix in the coconut.

3 Roll 1 heaped teaspoon of the mixture into a ball between the palms of your hands, then place on a prepared baking sheet and flatten slightly with a fork. Continue in this way until all the mixture is used up, spacing the biscuits 2.5 cm/1 inch apart to allow for spreading.

4 Bake in the oven for 15-20 minutes (see Cook's tip), until golden. Let the biscuits 'settle' for a few seconds, [!] then transfer to a wire rack with a palette knife. Leave to cool completely.

Cook's Notes

TIME
20 minutes preparation, 15-20 minutes baking.

COOK'S TIP
Swap the baking sheets halfway through cooking so the biscuits colour evenly.

WATCHPOINT
Do not leave the biscuits too long, or they may break when loosened.

●70 calories/300 kj per biscuit

Cheese hoops

MAKES 48

150 g/5oz plain flour
pinch of cayenne
pinch of salt
50 g/2 oz butter, diced
75 g/3 oz mature Cheddar cheese,
    finely grated (see Variation)
1 egg yolk
3 tablespoons water

1 Sift the flour, cayenne and salt into a bowl. Add the butter and rub it in until the mixture resembles fine breadcrumbs. Using a fork, stir in the grated Cheddar cheese. Make a well in centre.

2 Beat the egg yolk with the water, then pour into the well and mix to a soft dough with the fingers of one hand. Wrap in cling film and refrigerate for 30 minutes.

3 Heat the oven to 200C/400F/Gas 6.

4 On a lightly floured surface, roll out the dough to an 18 × 15 cm/ 7 × 6 inch rectangle. Trim edges, then cut the pastry lengthways into 24 strips. Cut the strips in half, to make a total of 48.

5 Shape each strip into a hoop and pinch the ends together to seal. Place the hoops on ungreased baking sheets. Bake just above and just below centre of oven for 15 mintes, or until set and lightly browned. Swap the sheets halfway through baking time so that the cheese hoops brown evenly.

6 Transfer the hoops to wire racks and leave to cool completely before serving (see Serving ideas).

BUNS & SCONES

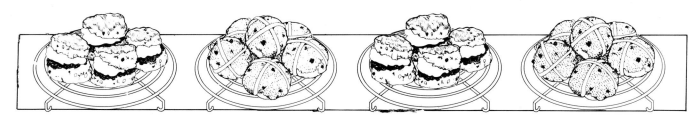

Date and oatmeal muffins

MAKES 16 SMALL MUFFINS

100 g/4 oz self-raising flour, sifted
1 teaspoon baking powder
pinch of salt
75 g/3 oz medium oatmeal
50 g/2 oz caster sugar
50 g/2 oz stoned dates, finely
   chopped
1 tablespoon golden syrup
15 g/½ oz margarine or butter
150 ml/¼ pint milk

1 Heat the oven to 200C/400F/Gas 6. Grease sixteen 6.5 cm/2½ inch patty or muffin moulds (see Cook's tip).
2 Put the dry ingredients into a bowl with the dates and stir well to mix. Make a well in the centre.
3 Stir the syrup, margarine and

milk together in a saucepan over low heat until the fat has melted, then pour into the dry ingredients and beat until smoothly blended.
4 Divide the mixture equally between the prepared moulds, then bake in the oven for 15-20 minutes until well-risen and springy.
5 Serve split and buttered while still warm (see Serving ideas).

Cook's Notes

TIME
25 minutes preparation, plus 15-20 minutes in the oven.

SERVING IDEAS
For a special occasion, split and spread with spiced butter (made by beating a little ground mixed spice and brown sugar into butter), honey or cream.

COOK'S TIP
Patty or muffin moulds come in trays of 6, 8 or

12. They are deeper than ordinary tartlet or bun tins, and have flat bottoms and sloping (not rounded) sides.

FREEZING
Cool the muffins quickly on a wire rack, then wrap in foil or place in a rigid container. Seal, label and freeze for up to 4 months. To serve: reheat from frozen, in foil, in an oven heated to 200C/400F/Gas 6 for 15 minutes.

●80 calories/325 kj per muffin

Spicy drop scones

MAKES 15-18
50 g/2 oz plain flour
pinch of salt
1 teaspoon baking powder
1 teaspoon ground mixed spice
50 g/2 oz plain wholemeal flour
25 g/1 oz caster sugar
1 egg, lightly beaten
175 ml/6 fl oz milk
25 g/1 oz butter, melted
lard, for frying

1 Sift the plain flour, salt, baking powder and spice into a bowl. Stir in the wholemeal flour and sugar, then make a well in the centre.
2 Add the egg, milk and melted butter and whisk together to make a smooth, fairly thick batter.
3 Lightly grease a large heavy-based frying-pan or girdle with lard and place over moderate heat (see Cook's tips).

4 Using a large metal spoon, drop 3-4 spoonfuls of the batter on to the hot pan taking care not to overcook it (see Cook's tips). Cook for 1-2 minutes, until the bubbles rise and burst on the surface, then turn each scone over with a palette knife and cook on the other side for 30-60 seconds until a deep golden brown (see Cook's tips).

5 Remove the cooked scones from the pan, wrap in a clean tea-towel and place on a wire rack. Continue making scones until all the batter is used. Stir the batter frequently and grease the pan lightly with more lard as necessary.
6 Serve the scones as soon as they are all cooked and while still warm (see Serving ideas).

Cook's Notes

TIME
Preparation and cooking take 30 minutes.

SERVING IDEAS
These spicy drop scones are delicious with butter and jam or honey; for an extravagant treat, top them with a swirl of whipped cream.

COOK'S TIPS
To test the temperature, drop a teaspoon of batter on to the pan: it should begin to bubble within 1 minute. If not, heat the pan a little longer.

For round scones, drop the batter from the tip of the spoon; for an oval shape, let it run off the side. Space each spoonful well apart or the batter will run together.

Press the scones gently with the flat side of the knife: if they are cooked, no batter will run out of the sides.

●55 calories/225 kj per scone

Welsh cakes

MAKES 16 CAKES

225 g/8 oz self-raising flour
½ teaspoon ground mixed spice
pinch of salt
50 g/2 oz margarine, diced
50 g/2 oz lard, diced
75 g/3 oz caster sugar
75 g/3 oz currants
1 egg
1 tablespoon milk
vegetable oil, for greasing

1 Sift the flour, spice and salt into a bowl. Add the margarine and lard and rub them in until the mixture resembles fine breadcrumbs. Stir in the sugar and currants.

2 Beat the egg with the milk, then stir into the flour mixture to make a firm dough. !

3 Roll out the dough on a lightly floured surface until 5 mm/¼ inch thick, then cut out as many rounds as possible using a 7 cm/2½ inch pastry cutter. Knead the trimmings lightly together, roll out and cut into more rounds, until there are 16 rounds altogether.

4 Heat the oven to 110C/225F/Gas ¼.

5 Grease a frying-pan or griddle with oil, then set over moderate heat until it is hot. Lower the heat, add a batch of cakes to the pan and fry for 3-4 minutes until golden brown on the undersides. Turn the cakes and fry them for a further 3-4 minutes on the other side.

6 Drain the cakes on absorbent paper, transfer to a serving platter and keep hot in the oven. Continue frying the remaining cakes in the same way, regreasing the pan between each batch.

7 Serve at once, while still hot (see Serving ideas).

Cook's Notes

TIME
Preparing and cooking take 30 minutes.

DID YOU KNOW
Most Welsh families will have their own favourite recipe, handed down through the generations, for Welsh cakes. They are often referred to as 'bakestones', the name used for the thick iron griddle on which they are traditionally cooked.

! WATCHPOINT
Do not allow the dough to become too wet, otherwise it will be difficult to roll out. You may not have to add all the milk.

SERVING IDEAS
Welsh cakes should be served hot. They are delicious sprinkled with caster sugar or spread with butter.

●135 calories/550 kj per cake

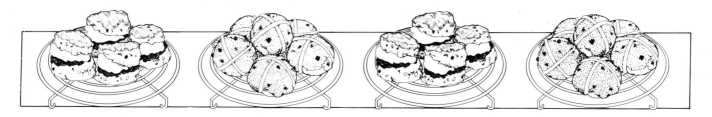

Apricot scone round

MAKES 6 WEDGES

50 g/2 oz dried apricots, chopped
225 g/8 oz plain flour
1 tablespoon baking powder
½ teaspoon salt
½ teaspoon ground cinnamon
50 g/2 oz light soft brown sugar
50 g/2 oz margarine or butter, diced
about 150 ml/¼ pint milk
milk, for glazing
margarine or butter, for greasing

1 Heat the oven to 220C/425F/Gas 7. Grease a baking sheet.

2 Sift the flour, baking powder, salt and cinnamon into a bowl. Stir in the sugar. Add the margarine and rub it in until the mixture resembles fine breadcrumbs. Stir in the apricots. Make a well in centre.

3 Add most of the milk and mix it in with a round-bladed knife, adding the remaining milk if necessary to give a soft, but not sticky dough. ☐ Gather the dough together with your fingers, turn out on to a lightly floured surface and knead briefly until smooth. Shape into a ball, then gently press out to a round, about 1 cm/½ inch thick. ☐

4 Place the scone round on the baking sheet and brush the top with milk. Using the point of a floured knife, mark into 6 equal wedges. Bake in the oven for 20-25 minutes until well risen and browned.

5 Cool, then pull the wedges apart and serve warm.

Cook's Notes

TIME
Preparation takes about 10 minutes, baking time is 20-25 minutes.

WATCHPOINT
Add only enough milk to bind the dry ingredients together: too much milk makes the dough sticky; too little gives a dry, crumbly dough.

The baking powder begins to work as soon as it is moistened, so the dough must be shaped and baked without delay.

●260 calories/1100 kj per wedge

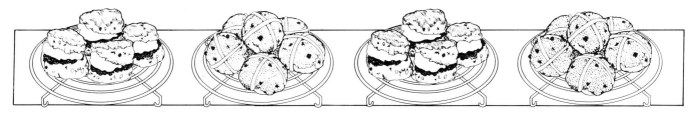

Nutty butterscotch buns

MAKES 9
280 g/10 oz sachet white bread mix
50 g/2 oz butter
185 ml/6½ fl oz hand-hot milk
50 g/2 oz light soft brown sugar

TOPPING
25 g/1 oz butter
50 g/2 oz light soft brown sugar
25 g/1 oz hazelnuts, toasted,
 skinned and finely chopped
1 tablespoon golden syrup

1 Make the topping: put the butter, sugar, nuts and syrup into a small saucepan and stir over low heat until the butter has melted and the sugar has dissolved. Pour into a 5 cm/2 inch deep, 18 cm/7 inch square tin. Set aside.

2 Put the bread mix in a bowl. Dice half the butter, add to the bread mix and rub in. Pour in the hand-hot milk and mix to a smooth dough. Turn out the dough on to a lightly floured surface and knead for about 5 minutes. Roll out to a 35 × 23 cm/14 × 9 inch rectangle.

3 Melt the remaining butter in a small pan, then brush it over the dough. Sprinkle over the sugar. Starting from 1 short side, roll up the dough like a Swiss roll. Arrange the finished roll so that the seamed side is at the bottom.

4 Cut the roll into 9 equal-sized slices. Lay slices (see Preparation) in the cake tin on top of nutty mixture. Cover with oiled polythene and leave to rise in a warm place for about 1 hour, until it is double in size.

5 Heat the oven to 200C/400F/Gas 6.

6 Uncover the buns and bake in the oven for about 25 minutes, until golden brown. Cool for 5 minutes, then turn out on to a serving plate so that the nutty mixture is on top. Serve hot or cold on their own, or with custard as a dessert (see Serving ideas).

Cook's Notes

TIME
20 minutes preparation, then 1 hour rising and 25 minutes baking.

SERVING IDEAS
The buns are pulled apart to serve: they make a delicious treat to offer with morning coffee or with custard as a dessert.

●230 calories/950 kj per portion

PREPARATION

Arrange bun slices in 3 rows on the butterscotch topping.

Cheese and bacon scones

MAKES 12

2 back bacon rashers, rinds
   removed
225 g/8 oz self-raising flour
1 teaspoon baking powder
1 teaspoon mustard powder
pinch of salt
pinch of cayenne pepper
50 g/2 oz margarine, diced
150 g/5 oz Cheddar cheese, finely
   grated
125 ml/4 fl oz milk
milk, for glazing
margarine, for greasing

1 Heat the oven to 220C/425F/Gas 7.
Lightly grease a large baking sheet.
2 Grill the bacon rashers for 2-3
minutes on each side, then leave to
cool.
3 Sift the flour, baking powder,
mustard powder, salt and cayenne
pepper into a large bowl. Add the
margarine and rub it in with your
fingertips until the mixture
resembles fine breadcrumbs. Using
kitchen scissors, snip the bacon into
the mixture. Add 100 g/4 oz of the
grated cheese and stir well to mix.
4 Add the milk, then mix quickly
[!] to a soft dough with a round-
bladed knife. Form the dough into a
ball, turn out on to a lightly floured
surface and knead briefly until free
of cracks.
5 Cut the dough in half. With
floured hands, shape each piece into
a ball, then pat out to a round, about
12 cm/5 inches in diameter and 2
cm/¾ inch thick. Cut each round
into 6 equal wedges. [!]
6 Brush the tops with milk and
sprinkle with the remaining cheese.
Place on prepared baking sheet,
about 2.5 cm/1 inch apart. Bake the
scones in the oven for 10-12
minutes, until well risen and
golden. Cool on a wire rack.

Cook's Notes

TIME
30 minutes to prepare,
10-12 minutes baking.

WATCHPOINTS
Mix the dough as quick-
ly as possible and handle
it lightly; overworking and
heavy handling produces
tough, heavy scones.
  Dip the blade of the knife in
flour before you cut the scone
wedges, otherwise it will stick
and give a ragged edge.

SERVING IDEAS
Eat these savoury scones,
warm or cold. They are
delicious split open, thickly
buttered and served with soup.

FREEZING
Wrap the cold scones in
a polythene bag, seal,
label and freeze for 2 months.
Defrost, in wrappings, at room
temperature for about 2 hours.

●165 calories/700 kj per scone

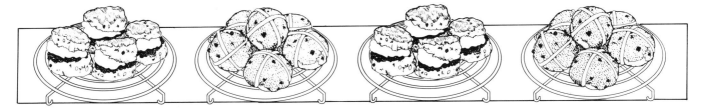

Honey cinnamon pinwheels

MAKES 8

225 g/8 oz self-raising flour
40 g/1½ oz margarine, diced
1½ tablespoons caster sugar
150 ml/¼ pint milk
1 tablespoon clear honey, to
    decorate
vegetable oil, for greasing

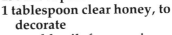

FILLING
15 g/½ oz margarine
2 tablespoons clear honey
1 teaspoon ground cinnamon
    (see Did you know)

1 Heat the oven to 200C/400F/Gas 6. Brush the bottom and sides of an 18 cm/7 inch sandwich tin with oil, then line the base with greaseproof paper and brush with oil.

2 Make the filling: in a small bowl, beat the margarine with the honey and the cinnamon until blended.

3 Sift the flour into a bowl, add the margarine and rub it in until the mixture begins to resemble fine breadcrumbs. Stir in the sugar and make a well in the centre.

4 Pour the milk into the well, then gradually draw the flour into the liquid to form a soft dough. Turn the dough on to a floured surface and roll out to a 20 cm/8 inch square.

5 Spread the honey mixture over the dough to cover completely then roll up like a Swiss roll. Cut the roll into 8 even-sized slices.

6 Put one slice in centre of the prepared tin, cut-side down, then arrange the remaining slices around it (see Preparation).

7 Bake in the oven for 30 minutes or until well risen and golden brown. Remove from the oven and turn out on to a wire rack with a plate placed underneath. To decorate: trickle the honey over the top, allowing excess to fall on to the plate.

8 Transfer to a serving plate, cut the pinwheels apart and serve warm or leave until completely cold.

Cook's Notes

 TIME
20 minutes preparation, 30 minutes baking.

 DID YOU KNOW
Cinnamon is the bark of a small evergreen tree which is a member of the laurel family. The bark is peeled from the branches and dried in the sun to form curled-up rolls. Cinnamon is difficult to grind and is usually bought ready ground for use in sweet dishes and cakes. It quickly becomes stale so should be bought in small quantities and not stored for a long time.

PREPARATION
To make the pinwheel shape in the cake tin:

Put one slice of dough in centre of the lined tin. Arrange remainder in a wheel around it.

●190 calories/800 kj per portion

Rum babas

MAKES 8

100 g/4 oz strong white flour
pinch of salt
1 teaspoon easy-blend dried yeast
50 ml/2 fl oz hand-hot milk
2 small eggs, beaten
50 g/2 oz margarine or butter,
    melted and cooled
25 g/1 oz currants
vegetable oil, for greasing
plain flour, for dusting

SYRUP
225 ml/8 fl oz water
75 g/3 oz sugar
4½ teaspoons lemon juice
2 cloves
65 ml/2½ fl oz dark rum

TO GLAZE AND DECORATE
4 tablespoons apricot jam
1 tablespoon water
150 ml/¼ pint double cream,
    whipped
4 glacé cherries, halved
16 'diamonds' of angelica

1 Brush eight 9 cm/3½ inch individual ring tins with oil and dust lightly with flour, shaking off any excess.
2 Sift the flour and salt into a large bowl, then sprinkle in the yeast and stir well to mix.
3 In a separate bowl, mix together the milk, eggs and margarine and gradually beat into the flour mixture to make a smooth batter. Stir in the currants until well dispersed.
4 Spoon the batter into the oiled ring tins (it should not come more than one-third of the way up), cover with oiled polythene and leave in a warm place for 30 minutes until the batter has risen to the top of the ring tins.
5 Meanwhile, heat the oven to 200C/400F/Gas 6.
6 Uncover the babas and bake in the oven for 15 minutes, until golden brown on top.
7 Turn the tins upside down on a work surface, leave for 10 minutes, then carefully ease the babas out of tins. Leave to cool slightly.
8 Meanwhile, prepare the syrup: put the water, sugar, lemon juice

and cloves into a heavy-based saucepan. Heat until the sugar has dissolved, then bring slowly to the boil. Remove the syrup from the heat and stir in the rum.
9 Put the babas into a large shallow dish and prick them all over with a fine skewer. Pour over the hot syrup and leave for 30 minutes to soak up the syrup.
10 Make the glaze: sieve the jam

into a small, heavy-based saucepan. Add the water and heat gently, stirring constantly, until the jam has melted. Remove glaze from heat and brush over the babas while still hot. Arrange babas on a serving plate or on individual plates.
11 To serve: spoon or pipe the whipped cream into the centre of each baba, then top with half a cherry and 2 'diamonds' of angelica.

Cook's Notes

TIME
50 minutes preparation; 15 minutes to bake and make syrup; 40 minutes to cool and soak; 15 minutes to finish.

VARIATION
If you do not have the small ring tins, you can use 150 ml/¼ pint dariole moulds instead.

DID YOU KNOW
Although the origin of rum baba is uncertain, many people do attribute its invention to a King Stanislas of Poland. One of the king's favourite stories was the fable Ali Baba: it is believed he called the cake after the story's hero.

●290 calories/1200 kj per baba

Orange iced buns

MAKES 8

280 g/10 oz packet white bread mix
finely grated zest of 1 large orange
25 g/1 oz caster sugar
200 ml/7 fl oz hand-hot water
vegetable oil, for greasing

TO DECORATE
175 g/6 oz icing sugar
4½ teaspoons strained orange juice
few drops of orange food colouring
crystallized orange slices (optional)

1 Oil a large baking sheet or tray.
2 Put the bread mix into a bowl, then stir in the orange zest and caster sugar and mix thoroughly. Add the water and mix well, first with a wooden spoon and then with your hand to make a firm dough.
3 Turn the dough out on to a lightly floured surface and knead for 5 minutes, then divide into 8 equal pieces. Shape each piece into a round, then roll out each round to an oval, about 10 cm/4 inches long.
4 Transfer the oval buns to the prepared sheet, spacing them well apart. Cover with oiled polythene and leave in a warm place for about 1 hour, or until the oval buns are

risen and have doubled in bulk.
5 About 20 minutes before the buns are risen, heat the oven to 220C/425F/Gas 7.
6 Uncover the buns and bake in the oven for 15 minutes, or until golden brown (see Cook's tips). Transfer the buns to a wire rack and leave to cool completely. ✱
7 Make the icing: sift the icing sugar into a bowl, then stir in the orange juice (see Cook's tips). Tint pale orange with food colouring.
8 Spread a little icing over the top of each bun. Decorate, if liked, then leave the buns for about 30 minutes, or until the orange icing is firm and set (see Cook's tips).

Wheatmeal Chelsea buns

MAKES 8

125 ml/4 fl oz milk
1 egg, beaten
225 g/8 oz brown or wheatmeal
  flour
½ teaspoon salt
25 g/1 oz butter, diced
25 g/1 oz light soft brown sugar
½ teaspoon ground mixed spice
  (optional)
7 g/¼ oz sachet easy-blend dried
  yeast
75 g/3 oz icing sugar
vegetable oil, for greasing

FILLING
75 g/3 oz currants
25 g/1 oz cut mixed peel
50 g/2 oz light soft brown sugar
½ teaspoon ground mixed spice
50 g/2 oz butter, melted

1 Heat the milk in a pan until warm, then beat in the egg and set aside until required. Grease a 20 cm/8 inch sandwich cake tin.
2 Sift the flour and salt into a large bowl. Add the butter and rub in until the mixture resembles fine breadcrumbs. Stir in the sugar, spice and yeast, make a well in the centre and pour in the milk mixture. Using a fork, mix to a soft dough.
3 Turn the dough out on to a lightly floured surface and knead for about 10 minutes, until smooth. !
4 Shape the dough into a ball and place in a large oiled bowl. Cover with oiled polythene and leave to rise in a warm place for 1-1½ hours or until doubled in size.
5 Meanwhile, make the filling: mix the currants with the peel, sugar and spice, then pour over the melted butter and stir well.
6 Uncover the risen dough and turn out on to a floured surface. Knead gently until the dough is back to original size, then roll into a 30 × 23 cm/12 × 9 inch rectangle. Pour the filling over the rectangle and spread it out to cover dough.
7 Starting at a short edge, roll up like a Swiss roll, to enclose the filling. Brush the end with water and press firmly to seal, then slice across into 8 pieces.
8 Place 1 piece, cut-side up, in the centre of the prepared tin. Arrange the remaining pieces around it so that they are just touching. Cover with oiled polythene and leave in a warm place for 45 minutes or until the buns have risen.
9 Heat the oven to 200C/400F/Gas 6.
10 Bake the buns in the oven for about 30 minutes until risen and golden brown. Transfer to a wire rack and leave to cool completely.
11 Make the icing: sift the icing sugar into a bowl, then stir in enough water to give a smooth coating consistency. Drizzle the icing over the top of the cooled buns before serving.

Cook's Notes

TIME
30 minutes preparation, 1¾-2¼ hours rising and about 30 minutes baking, plus cooling time.

WATCHPOINT
The dough will be very sticky: do not add any extra flour to it; just continue kneading until dough becomes soft, pliable and elastic.

●290 calories/1225 kj per bun

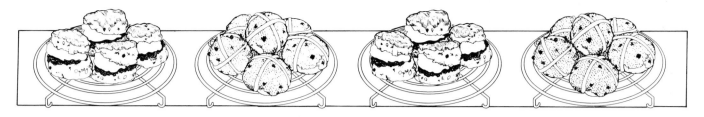

Cornbread muffins

MAKES 12

100 g/4 oz yellow cornmeal (see Buying guide)

175 g/6 oz plain flour, sifted
50 g/2 oz caster sugar
2 teaspoons baking powder
1 teaspoon salt
1 large egg, lightly beaten
350 ml/12 fl oz milk
50 g/2 oz margarine or butter, melted
margarine, for greasing

1 Heat the oven to 200C/400F/Gas 6. Brush 12 deep bun or patty tins lightly all over with margarine (see Cook's tip).
2 Sift the dry ingredients together into a bowl and make a well in the centre.

3 Mix together the egg, milk and melted margarine and pour into the well. Using a balloon whisk, combine swiftly with a few strokes. [!]
4 Spoon the batter into the prepared tins, filling them two-thirds full. Bake in the oven for 20-25 minutes until golden.
5 Allow the muffins to cool slightly in the tins, then run a knife around the edge of the tins and turn out on to a wire rack. Serve warm.

Cook's Notes

 TIME
Preparation takes about 15 minutes, baking in the oven 20-25 minutes.

 SERVING IDEAS
Cornbread muffins are traditionally served with gammon in Canada, but they are delicious to eat in a variety of ways. Try them instead of toast for Sunday breakfast, or serve them buttered for tea, with jam.

●155 calories/635 kj per muffin

BUYING GUIDE
Cornmeal is available in packets from supermarkets and health food stores.

 WATCHPOINT
Avoid overmixing the batter: this will destroy the light texture of the muffins.

COOK'S TIP
If you do not have patty or bun tins, use a 20 cm/8 inch square baking tin and cut the cornbread into 5 cm/2 inch squares when baked.

132

Hot cross buns

MAKES 12

150 ml/¼ pint milk
4 tablespoons water
1 large egg
500 g/1 lb strong white flour
1 teaspoon salt
50 g/2 oz butter, diced
50 g/2 oz caster sugar
1 teaspoon ground mixed spice
½ teaspoon ground cinnamon
½ teaspoon freshly grated nutmeg
175 g/6 oz currants
50 g/2 oz cut mixed peel
2 × 7 g/¼ oz sachets easy-blend
  dried yeast
vegetable oil, for greasing
50 g/2 oz sugar and 4 tablespoons
  water, to glaze

PASTRY CROSSES
50 g/2 oz plain flour
about 2 tablespoons water

1 Heat the milk and water in a pan until warm, then pour into a jug. Beat in the egg and set aside. Grease 2 large baking sheets.
2 Sift the flour and salt into a warmed, large bowl. Add the butter and rub it in with your fingertips. Stir in the sugar, spices, currants and peel, then stir in the yeast. Pour in the milk mixture and then mix to a soft dough.
3 Turn the dough out on to a lightly floured surface and knead for about 10 minutes, or until it is elastic. [!]
4 Shape into a ball and place in an oiled large bowl. Cover with oiled polythene and leave to rise in a warm place for 1½-2 hours or until the dough has doubled in size.
5 Uncover the risen dough and turn out on to a floured surface. Punch down the dough with your knuckles, then knead for 2 minutes. Divide into 12 pieces and shape each into a round.
6 Place the rounds, well apart, on the baking sheets. Cover with oiled polythene and leave to rise in a warm place for 30-40 minutes or until almost doubled in size.
7 About 20 minutes before the rounds are risen, heat the oven to 220C/425F/Gas 7. Then make the crosses: sift the flour into a bowl and

stir in just enough water to make a firm dough. Knead gently on a floured surface until smooth, then roll out and cut into 24 strips, each 7.5 cm × 5 mm/3 × ¼ inch.
8 Uncover the buns. Brush underside of pastry strips with water and place 2 strips on top of each bun to form a cross. Bake in the oven for 15-20 minutes, until risen and golden brown. Transfer to a wire rack, placed over a tray.
9 Make the glaze: heat the sugar and water in a saucepan, stirring until the sugar has dissolved. Brush over the warm buns. Leave the buns to cool completely.

Cook's Notes

TIME
30-40 minutes preparation, 2-2¾ hours rising and 15-20 minutes baking, plus cooling time.

WATCHPOINT
The dough should be stickier than a plain bread dough. Do not knead in too much flour, or the buns will have a heavy texture.

● 290 calories/1200 kj per bun

Doughnut dreams

SERVES 4

4 ring doughnuts, sliced in half horizontally

100 ml/3½ fl oz milk, at room temperature

40 g/1½ oz packet dessert topping mix with cream added (see Buying guide)

1-2 drops vanilla essence

225 g/8 oz can pineapple pieces in syrup, drained

75 g/3 oz sugar

3 tablespoons water

4 'diamonds' of angelica, to decorate

1 Pour the milk into a bowl. Sprinkle in the topping mix, then add the vanilla essence and whisk until stiff.

2 Set aside 3-4 tablespoons of the topping mixture, then fold in all but 4 of the pineapple pieces. Use the mixture to sandwich the doughnut halves back together. Refrigerate the doughnuts until required.

3 Place the sugar and water in a small, heavy-based saucepan [!] and heat gently, without stirring, until the sugar has dissolved. Bring slowly to the boil and boil for about 5 minutes, until the syrup turns a pale golden colour. Remove from the heat.

4 Place the filled doughnuts on a wire rack with a piece of greaseproof paper underneath. Pour the caramelized syrup straight from the pan over the top of each doughnut and allow it to run down the sides. Leave for 2-3 minutes to set.

5 Pipe or spoon the reserved topping mix into the centre of each doughnut, then decorate with a piece of pineapple and a 'diamond' of angelica.

Iced cup cakes

MAKES 20

150 g/5 oz self-raising flour
100 g/4 oz soft-tub margarine
100 g/4 oz caster sugar
2 eggs
2-3 drops vanilla flavouring

ICING AND DECORATION
225 g/8 oz icing sugar
2-3 tablespoons warm water
1-2 drops vanilla flavouring
few drops of food colouring
    (optional)
sugar strands, sugar flowers or
    other cake decorations, to finish

1 Heat the oven to 180C/350F/Gas 4. Stand 20 paper cup cake cases in tart moulds (see Cook's tips).
2 Sift the flour into a large bowl. Add the margarine, caster sugar, eggs and vanilla, then beat with a wooden spoon for 1-2 minutes, until evenly blended.

3 Divide the mixture equally between the paper cases (see Cook's tips). Bake in the centre and just above the centre of the oven for about 15 minutes, until golden and springy to the touch. Swap the tart tins halfway through baking time so the cakes cook evenly.
4 Lift the cakes, in their cases, on to a wire rack and leave to cool completely (see Cook's tips).

5 Make the icing: sift the icing sugar into a bowl, then stir in just enough water to give a smooth coating consistency. Stir in the vanilla, then tint the icing a pastel colour with colouring, if liked.
6 Using a small palette knife, spread the icing over the tops of the cakes. Sprinkle with decorations while the icing is still soft, then leave to set before serving.

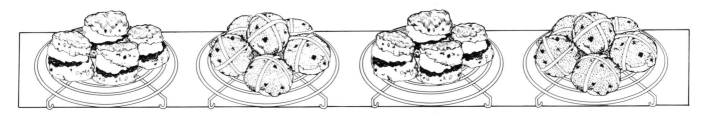

Sponge drops

MAKES 12-14
2 large eggs, beaten
100 g/4 oz caster sugar
1-2 drops vanilla flavouring
100 g/4 oz plain flour
1 teaspoon baking powder
extra caster sugar, for dredging
vegetable oil, for greasing

TO SERVE
100-175 g/4-6 oz strawberry jam
300 ml/½ pint double cream
little extra caster sugar, to finish
(optional)

1 Heat the oven to 190C/375F/Gas 5.
Grease 2 large baking sheets.
2 Put the eggs, caster sugar and
vanilla flavouring in a large heatproof bowl. Set bowl over a pan half
full of gently simmering water.
3 Using a rotary or hand-held
electric whisk, beat together until
the mixture is thick and foamy.
Continue beating until the mixture
is thick enough to hold the trail of
the whisk for 3 seconds when the
beaters are lifted.
4 Remove the bowl from the pan
and whisk for a few minutes more
until the mixture is cool. Sift the
flour with the baking powder, then
fold into the egg mixture about one-
third at a time, using a large metal
spoon.
5 Put the mixture, a teaspoonful at a
time, on to the prepared baking
sheets. Space the spoonfuls about
2.5 cm/1 inch apart to allow room for
spreading. Sift a little caster sugar
over the top of the drops, then bake
in the oven for 10 minutes.
6 Stand each baking sheet on a
damp tea-towel for 30 seconds, then
remove the drops with a palette
knife and transfer to a wire rack.
Leave to cool completely.
7 To serve: turn the drops upside
down so that the flat base is
uppermost. Spread half the drops
with jam. Whip the cream until

thick, then either pipe or spoon a
swirl of cream on each of the
remaining drops. Sandwich

together in pairs. Sift the extra caster
sugar, if using, and sprinkle a little
over the top of each drop.

Cook's Notes

TIME
30-40 minutes prepara-
tion (depending on the
type of whisk used); baking
takes 10 minutes. Allow about
30 minutes for cooling and
filling.

FREEZING
The unfilled drops can
be frozen: pack in a rigid
container with waxed paper
between layers and freeze for up
to 10 months. Defrost at room
temperature for about 2 hours
before filling.

VARIATION
For chocolate drops,
replace 1 tablespoon
flour with the same amount of
cocoa powder. Sift the cocoa
with the flour and baking
powder.

STORAGE
Once assembled, the
drops should be served
as soon as possible. The unfilled drops can be stored
overnight in an airtight tin.

● 205 calories/850 kj each pair

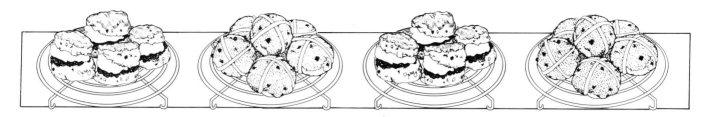

Apricot and walnut tea buns

chopped walnuts. Stir in the egg.
3 Divide the mixture equally between the prepared moulds, then lightly rough up each surface with back of a fork. Bake for about 20 min-

utes, or until risen, and browned.
4 Cool the buns for 5 minutes, then remove from the moulds. Leave on a wire rack to cool completely before serving (see Cook's tip).

MAKES 12

225 g/8 oz self-raising flour
1 teaspoon ground cinnamon
100 g/4 oz margarine, diced
100 g/4 oz light soft brown sugar
50 g/2 oz dried apricots, finely chopped
25 g/1 oz shelled walnuts, finely chopped
1 large egg, lightly beaten
vegetable oil, for greasing

1 Heat the oven to 200C/400F/Gas 6. Brush 12 bun moulds with oil.
2 Sift the flour and cinnamon into a large bowl. Add the margarine and rub it in until the mixture resembles fine crumbs. Using a fork, stir in the brown sugar, chopped apricots and

Cook's Notes

TIME
15 minutes preparation, 20 minutes baking, plus about 1 hour to cool.

 FREEZING
Pack the buns in a rigid container with waxed paper between layers; seal tightly and freeze for up to 3 months. To serve: defrost the buns at room temperature for about 2 hours, then unpack and place on a serving plate.

●185 calories/775 kj per bun

COOK'S TIP
The buns are nicest eaten on the day of making. Any left over can be stored in an airtight container for up to 2 days; alternatively, they can be frozen (see left).

VARIATION
Sift 5 tablespoons icing sugar into a bowl, then stir in enough strained lemon juice to give a smooth coating consistency. Trickle the icing over the buns. Leave for 15-20 minutes to set before serving.

137

Devonshire splits

MAKES 9
225 g/8 oz strong white flour
¼ teaspoon salt
1 teaspoon easy-blend dried yeast
150 ml/¼ pint milk
25 g/1 oz margarine or butter
1 tablespoon sugar
vegetable oil, for greasing

FILLING
4-5 tablespoons red jam
150 ml/¼ pint double cream,
   whipped until forming soft peaks
little icing sugar, for dusting

1 Sift the flour and salt into a large bowl, then stir in the yeast.
2 Warm the milk with the margarine and sugar over very low heat, stirring until the margarine is melted, ☐ then pour on to the flour mixture. Using a wooden spoon, mix to a soft dough, then beat until the dough comes away from the sides of the bowl.
3 Turn out on to a well-floured surface and knead for about 10 minutes, until smooth and elastic. Shape into a ball and place in a clean, oiled bowl. Cover bowl with cling film or oiled polythene and leave in a warm place for about 1 hour, until the dough is risen and doubled in bulk.
4 Oil a large baking sheet. Turn the dough out on to a lightly floured surface and knead briefly, then divide into 9 equal pieces. Shape each piece into a ball and place on the prepared baking sheet. Cover with oiled polythene or place in an oiled, large polythene bag. Leave in a warm place for about 40 minutes, until the buns are risen and puffy.
5 Meanwhile, heat the oven to 220C/425F/Gas 7.
6 Uncover the buns and bake in the oven for about 10 minutes, until cooked. Wrap the buns in a clean tea-towel and leave to cool completely.
7 To serve: split and fill with jam and cream (see Preparation), then sift icing sugar over the tops.

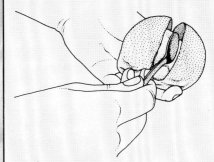

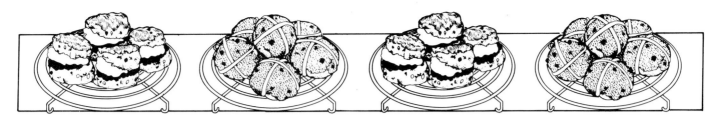

Sweet bun ring

MAKES 10

350 g/12 oz strong white flour
½ teaspoon salt
25 g/1 oz margarine or butter
25 g/1 oz caster sugar
finely grated zest ½ small lemon
1½ teaspoons easy-blend dried
   yeast
4 tablespoons cold milk
150 ml/¼ pint hand-hot water
¼ teaspoon vanilla flavouring
vegetable oil, for greasing

GLAZE

25 g/1 oz sugar
2 tablespoons water
1-2 teaspoons sesame seeds, to
   decorate

1 Sift the flour and salt into a bowl. Add the margarine and rub it into the flour with your fingertips. Mix in the sugar, lemon zest and the easy-blend yeast.

2 Mix together the milk, water and vanilla and pour on to the flour mixture. Using a wooden spoon, mix to a soft dough. Turn out on to a well-floured surface and knead for about 10 minutes, until the dough is smooth and elastic.

3 Oil a large baking sheet. Divide the dough into 10 equal-sized pieces and shape into balls. Place in a ring on the prepared baking sheet, so that they are just touching one another.

4 Cover with oiled polythene and leave to rise in a warm place for about 1¼ hours, or until doubled in size.

5 Heat the oven to 200C/400F/Gas 6.

6 Make the glaze: put the sugar and water in a small saucepan and bring to the boil. Remove from the heat.

7 Uncover the bun ring and bake in the oven for 15-20 minutes until risen and browned. Using a palette knife, carefully loosen the buns without breaking the ring and transfer to a wire rack.

8 Brush the buns with the glaze, while they are still warm, then sprinkle with the sesame seeds. Leave to cool, then transfer the ring to a large serving platter (see Serving ideas).

Cook's Notes

TIME
Initial preparation is 25 minutes; 1¼ hours rising and 15-20 minutes baking, plus cooling.

SERVING IDEAS
Place a small glass dish of butter curls in the centre of the ring and provide a sharp knife to separate the buns.

● 165 calories/705 kj per bun

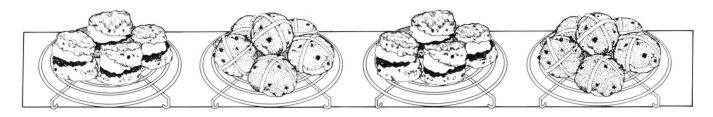

Singin' hinny

SERVES 8
225 g/8 oz self-raising flour
¼ teaspoon salt
½ teaspoon baking powder
75 g/3 oz lard, diced
25 g/1 oz caster sugar
50 g/2 oz currants
5-6 tablespoons milk
15-25 g/½-1 oz lard
butter, for serving

1 Sift the flour, salt and baking powder together. Add diced lard and rub it into the flour with your fingertips until the mixture resembles fine breadcrumbs.

2 Mix in the sugar, currants and enough milk to make a fairly soft but manageable dough (see Cook's tips).

3 Roll out the dough on a lightly floured surface to a round about 20 cm/8 inches in diameter. Using a sharp knife, cut the round of dough in half, if liked (see Cook's tips).

4 Heat 15 g/½ oz of the lard in a large, heavy frying-pan. Put dough in pan and cook over low heat for 10-15 minutes until the dough has risen. It should be cooked more than halfway through and be well browned underneath.

5 Lift the dough with a fish slice and add more lard to the pan, allowing it to melt and coat the pan base. Turn the hinny over, then gently lower it back into the pan. Continue cooking the hinny very gently for about 10 minutes or until brown on the underside. Check during cooking and lower the heat more, if necessary, to prevent the hinny over-browning and burning.

6 Using a fish slice, remove the hinny to a work surface or board. Split it in half horizontally while it is hot and spread with butter. Sandwich together again and cut into wedges. Serve at once, while still hot and buttery.

Cook's Notes

TIME
The hinny takes about 35 minutes to prepare and cook.

COOK'S TIPS
The hinny is best cooked as soon as the dough is made.
Cutting the dough will make it easier to turn in the pan.

DID YOU KNOW
This recipe is traditional to Northumberland and Durham where hinny is a term of endearment. The hinny was traditionally made on a girdle and would sizzle or 'sing' as it cooked.

VARIATION
Some traditional recipes include 50 g/2 oz ground rice in place of that amount of flour.

SERVING IDEAS
The hot hinny is particularly tasty when spread with cinnamon butter. To make the butter: mix 100 g/4 oz butter with 40 g/1½ oz caster sugar and 1 pinch cinnamon.

● 250 calories/1055 kj per portion

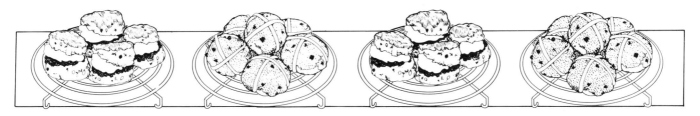

Sage and onion scones

MAKES ABOUT 8

40 g/1½ oz margarine or butter
1 large onion, finely chopped
100 g/4 oz wholemeal flour
125 g/4 oz self-raising flour
1 teaspoon baking powder
pinch of salt
1 tablespoon chopped fresh sage, or
   1½ teaspoons dried sage
1 large egg
4-5 tablespoons milk
vegetable oil, for greasing

1 Heat the oven to 220C/425F/Gas 7. Grease a baking sheet.
2 Melt 15 g/½ oz margarine in a frying-pan. Add the onion and fry gently for 10 minutes, until soft and browned. Remove the onion from the pan with a slotted spoon and reserve.
3 Sift the flours, baking powder and salt into a large bowl. Tip the bran left in the sieve into the bowl and stir well to mix. Dice the remaining margarine, then rub it into the flour mixture with your fingertips. Stir in the sage and fried onions, mixing well. Make a well in the centre.
4 Beat the egg with 4 tablespoons milk; add to the flour mixture and, using a round-bladed knife, mix to a soft dough, ! adding more milk if necessary. Form the dough into a ball, turn out on to a lightly floured surface and knead briefly until smooth.
5 Roll out the dough until 2 cm/¾ inch thick, then cut into as many rounds as possible with a 6.5 cm/2½ inch round cutter. Knead the trimmings lightly together, roll out again and cut into more rounds. You should make about 8 altogether.
6 Brush the tops of the scones lightly with milk, then transfer to the prepared baking sheet. ! Bake on the top shelf of the oven for about 20 minutes, until risen and browned. Cool on a wire rack (see Serving ideas).

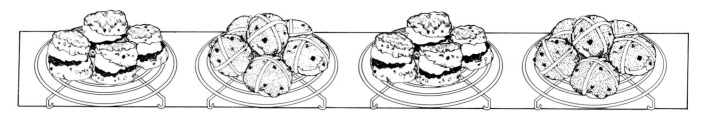

Soured cream girdle scones

MAKES 12

 225 g/8 oz plain flour
1 teaspoon bicarbonate of soda
 1 teaspoon cream of tartar
1 teaspoon salt
15 g/½ oz margarine or butter
15 g/½ oz caster sugar
300 ml/½ pint soured cream
lard, for greasing
butter, to serve

1 Sift the flour, bicarbonate of soda, cream of tartar and salt into a large bowl. Add the margarine and rub it in with your fingertips then stir in the caster sugar.

2 Using a fork, add enough soured cream to make a soft dough. Divide the dough in half, flour your hands lightly, then knead the dough lightly on a well-floured surface until smooth. [!]

3 Carefully shape the dough into 2 rounds, each about 1 cm/½ inch thick. Cut each round into 6 equal wedges.

4 Lightly grease a heavy frying-pan or girdle with lard and heat over moderate heat. [!] Pour away any excess lard, then cook the scones in batches for about 4-5 minutes on each side until golden and cooked through. Regrease the girdle with lard as necessary.

5 Cool the scones on a wire rack, for 20 minutes. Serve on the day of making, and spread each one generously with butter.

142

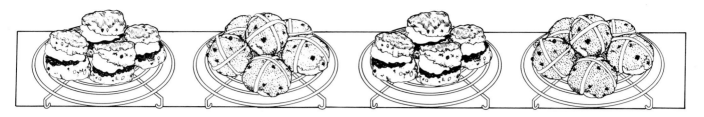

Devon scones

MAKES 7-8

225 g/8 oz plain flour
1 teaspoon cream of tartar
½ teaspoon bicarbonate of soda
½ teaspoon salt

50 g/2 oz margarine or butter, diced
125-150 ml/4-5 fl oz milk
vegetable oil, for greasing
extra plain flour

TO SERVE
3-4 tablespoons strawberry jam
125 g/4 oz clotted or double cream

1 Heat the oven to 230C/450F/Gas 8. Grease and lightly flour a large baking sheet.
2 Sift the flour with the cream of tartar, bicarbonate of soda and salt, then sift again into a large bowl. Add the diced margarine and rub it in until the mixture resembles fine breadcrumbs. Make a well in the centre.
3 Pour in most of the milk and mix to a soft (but not sticky) dough with a fork, adding a little more of the milk if necessary. Gather the dough into a ball, turn it out on to a lightly floured surface and knead it lightly and briefly until smooth.[!]
4 Either pat or lightly roll out the dough to a round about 1 cm/½ inch thick. Using a 7.5 cm/2½ inch round pastry cutter, cut out as many scones as possible (see Preparation). Lightly knead the trimmings together, pat or roll out again and cut out more scones.
5 Brush the tops of the scones with milk and place on the prepared baking sheet. Bake in the oven, just above the centre, for about 15 minutes until risen and browned. Wrap the scones in a clean tea-towel and leave to cool. [✳][!]
6 To serve, split each scone in half with your fingers, spread the bottom half with jam and the top with clotted cream, then lightly replace the top half.

Cook's Notes

 TIME
Preparation takes 10-15 minutes and baking about 15 minutes. Allow 30-45 minutes for cooling.

PREPARATION
For a good, neat shape, press the cutter down firmly and sharply, without twisting it; then lift it up and gently shake out the scone.

 WATCHPOINTS
The dough should be mixed quickly and handled as lightly as possible, otherwise the scones will be tough and heavy.

Scones do not keep well and should be eaten the day they are made. Any left over, however, can be toasted the following day.

 FREEZING
Cool quickly, then pack immediately in a polythene bag. Seal, label and freeze for up to 6 months. Defrost at room temperature for about 1 hour.

VARIATIONS
For tea-time scones, stir 1 tablespoon sugar and 50 g/2 oz currants or sultanas into the flour after rubbing in the margarine. Serve the scones buttered.

●310 calories/1300 kj per scone

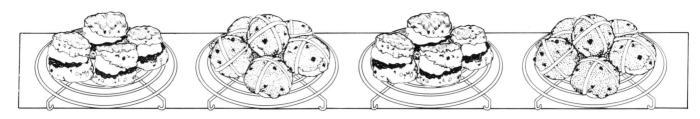

Lemon tops

MAKES 18

100 g/4 oz margarine, softened
100 g/4 oz light soft brown sugar
2 eggs, lightly beaten
finely grated zest of 1 lemon
100 g/4 oz self-raising flour, sifted

ICING AND DECORATION
50 g/2 oz butter, softened
100 g/4 oz icing sugar, sifted
2 teaspoons lemon juice
2-3 tablespoons lemon curd
18 small lemon jelly slices

1 Heat the oven to 180C/350F/Gas 4. Stand 18 paper cup cake cases in bun or tart moulds.
2 Beat the margarine and brown sugar until pale and fluffy. Add the eggs a little at a time, beating thoroughly after each addition. Beat

in the lemon zest. Using a large metal spoon, fold in the flour.
3 Divide the mixture equally between the paper cases, ⚠ spreading it as evenly as possible. Bake in the centre and just above centre of oven for 25-30 minutes, until risen and pale golden, swapping the trays after 15 minutes to ensure even cooking.
4 Cool the cakes for 5 minutes then transfer them, still in their paper cases, to a wire rack and leave for

about 1 hour to cool completely.
5 Meanwhile, make the icing: beat butter until very soft, then beat in icing sugar and lemon juice. Place the icing in a piping bag fitted with a small star nozzle and refrigerate until required.
6 Spread the top of each cake with lemon curd, almost to the edge. Pipe a border of small stars of icing around the top edge of each cake. Decorate each top with a lemon jelly slice. Serve as soon as possible.

Cook's Notes

TIME
15 minutes, then 25-30 minutes baking, plus cooling time for the cakes. Finishing takes 10-15 minutes.

WATCHPOINT
To ensure the cakes will be level, do not fill the cases more than half full.

VARIATIONS
Blackcurrant tops: make the icing with milk instead of lemon juice and spread the cakes with blackcurrant jam. Omit the jelly slices.
Orange tops: use orange zest, juice and curd instead of lemon.

● 145 calories/600 kj per cake

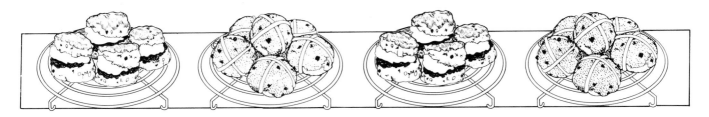

Sweet pumpkin scones

MAKES 10-12

275 g/10 oz self-raising flour
1 teaspoon salt
50 g/2 oz margarine, softened
50 g/2 oz caster sugar
5 tablespoons canned pumpkin
  purée (see Buying guide and
  Economy)
1 egg, lightly beaten
50 g/2 oz currants
2 tablespoons milk
little beaten egg or milk, to glaze
margarine, for greasing

1 Heat the oven to 220C/425F/Gas 7. Grease a large baking tray and dust with flour, shaking off the excess.
2 Sift the flour and salt into a bowl and set aside.
3 In a separate bowl, beat the margarine and sugar until pale and fluffy, then beat in pumpkin purée with 3 tablespoons of the flour (see Cook's tips). Add the egg and 1 more tablespoon sifted flour and beat until evenly blended. Stir in the currants. Using a fork, stir in the remaining flour. Add the milk and

mix with the fork to a soft dough.
4 Turn the dough on to a lightly floured surface and knead briefly, then roll out to a round about 1 cm/½ inch thick. Using a plain or fluted 5 cm/2 inch round cutter, cut the dough into as many rounds as possible (see Cook's tips).
5 Knead the trimmings lightly together, roll out and cut into more

rounds, to make 10-12 altogether. Transfer the rounds to the prepared baking tray and brush the tops with a little beaten egg or milk.
6 Bake the scones just above the centre of oven for 15-20 minutes, until risen, golden and just firm to the touch. Cool on a wire rack, then transfer to a serving plate and serve (see Serving ideas).

Cook's Notes

 TIME
30 minutes preparation, and 15-20 minutes baking, plus cooling time.

 COOK'S TIPS
The flour helps prevent the mixture curdling.
To stop the dough sticking, dip the cutter into plain flour before cutting each round.

 VARIATIONS
Sift ½-1 teaspoon ground mixed spice or cinnamon with the self-raising flour and the salt.
If pumpkin is not available use the same quantity of cooked and puréed carrot.

 BUYING GUIDE
Puréed pumpkin is available in cans from good delicatessens.

 ECONOMY
Left-over canned purée is delicious served as a vegetable accompaniment — heat it through gently, then season with salt, pepper, lemon juice and fresh herbs.

 SERVING IDEAS
Serve scones warm or cold, split, buttered and spread with jam or honey for a teatime treat.

●175 calories/725 kj per scone

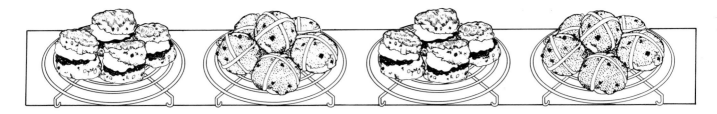

Jam buns

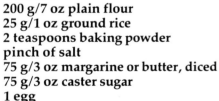

MAKES 8
200 g/7 oz plain flour
25 g/1 oz ground rice
2 teaspoons baking powder
pinch of salt
75 g/3 oz margarine or butter, diced
75 g/3 oz caster sugar
1 egg
2 tablespoons milk
2 tablespoons jam (see For children)
caster sugar, for dredging
vegetable oil, for greasing

1 Heat the oven to 200C/400F/Gas 6. Grease a large baking sheet and line the base with greaseproof paper then grease the paper.
2 Sift the flour, ground rice, baking powder and salt into a large bowl.

Add the margarine and rub it in with your fingertips, then stir in the sugar. Make a well in the centre. Beat the egg with the milk, then add to the dry ingredients and mix to a moist, but firm, dough.
3 Cut the dough into 8 equal pieces. With lightly floured hands, shape each piece into a ball. Make a hollow in the centre of each bun with your finger. Spoon a little jam into each

hollow, then pinch the edges of the dough together to seal.
4 Place the buns, sealed side down, on the prepared baking sheet. Bake in the oven, just above centre, for about 20 minutes, until risen, golden and just firm to the touch.
5 Cool the buns for 10-15 minutes, then transfer to a wire rack. Sprinkle with caster sugar and leave to cool completely. Serve fresh.

Cook's Notes

TIME
20 minutes preparation and 20 minutes baking, plus cooling time.

 WATCHPOINT
It is a good idea to line the baking sheet, just in case the jam leaks out of the buns during baking.

FOR CHILDREN
Raspberry jam is often used to fill these buns, but children will love the surprise of different jams hidden in the buns. You can try such jams as strawberry, apricot, plum and blackcurrant.

● 255 calories/1080 kj per bun

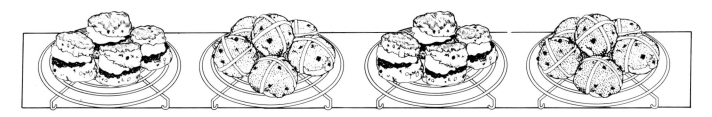

Butterfly cakes

MAKES 12
150 g/5 oz self-raising flour
pinch of salt
75 g/3 oz butter or margarine,
    softened
75 g/3 oz caster sugar
grated zest of 1 large orange
1 egg, beaten
2 tablespoons orange juice

BUTTERCREAM
100 g/4 oz butter or margarine,
    softened
225 g/8 oz icing sugar, sifted
about 2 tablespoons orange juice
few drops of orange food colouring
    (optional)

1 Heat the oven to 200C/400F/Gas 6.
Line each mould of a 12-mould tart
tin with a paper case (see Cook's
tips).

2 Sift the flour with the salt and
reserve. Beat the butter, sugar and
orange zest together until pale and
fluffy, then beat in the egg, a little at
a time. Using a large metal spoon,
fold in the sifted flour, then mix in
the orange juice.
3 Divide the mixture equally
between the paper cases. Bake in the
oven, above the centre, for about 15
minutes, until golden and springy
to the touch. Remove from the
moulds and leave on a wire rack to
cool completely.
4 Meanwhile, make the buttercream: beat the butter until very soft
and creamy. Gradually beat in all
but 1 teaspoon of the icing sugar,
adding sufficient orange juice to
give a smooth buttercream which
will hold its shape. Tint pale orange
with a few drops of food colouring,
if liked. Put into a piping bag fitted
with a star nozzle (see Cook's tips).
5 Cut a slice from the top of each
cake. Cut the slices in half and
reserve.
6 Pipe a large rosette of buttercream

on each cake, then replace the cake
slices at an angle on the buttercream
to resemble butterflies' wings. Sift
the reserved icing sugar over the
tops.

Cook's Notes

TIME
20-25 minutes prepara-
tion, 15 minutes baking,
plus cooling time. Finishing
takes about 5 minutes.

COOK'S TIPS
The moulds support the
cakes during baking and
help give a good round shape. If
you do not have a tart tin, use
double paper cases for each cake
and stand them on a baking tray
to give the necessary support.
    You can fork the buttercream
on to the cakes if you do not want
to pipe it.

●255 calories/1075 kj per cake

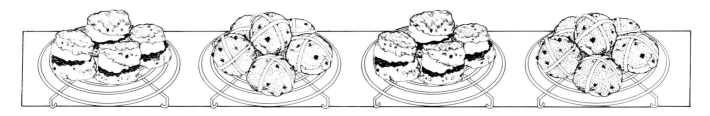

Sticky ginger buns

 MAKES 9

280 g/10 oz packet brown bread mix
50 g/2 oz butter
185 ml/6½ fl oz hand-hot milk
50 g/2 oz light soft brown sugar

TOPPING

25 g/1 oz butter
50 g/2 oz light soft brown sugar
25 g/1 oz drained stem ginger,
    chopped
1 tablespoon ginger syrup (from the
    jar)

1 Prepare the topping: put the butter, sugar, chopped ginger and syrup into a small saucepan and stir over low heat until the butter has melted and the sugar dissolved.

Pour into a 5 cm/2 inch deep, 18 cm/7 inch square tin and set aside while preparing the bun dough.

2 Place the bread mix in a bowl. Rub in half the butter, then pour in the milk and mix to a dough (see Cook's tips). Turn out the dough on to a floured surface and knead for 5 minutes, then roll out to a 35 × 23 cm/14 × 9 inch rectangle.

3 Melt the remaining butter in a small pan, then brush it over the dough. Sprinkle over the sugar. Starting from 1 short side, roll up the dough like a Swiss roll.

4 Cut the roll in 9 equal slices. Lay the slices, in 3 rows of 3, in the prepared tin so that 1 cut side rests on the ginger mixture. Cover with oiled polythene and leave to rise in a warm place for about 1 hour, until doubled in size. Meanwhile, heat the oven to 200C/400F/Gas 6.

5 Uncover the buns and bake in the oven for about 25 minutes, until

golden brown. Cool for 5 minutes then turn out on to a serving plate or board, so that the ginger mixture is on top. Cut apart to serve (see Cook's tips).

Cook's Notes

TIME
20 minutes preparation, then 1 hour rising and 25 minutes baking.

COOK'S TIPS
Keeping the dough warm ensures the yeast expands it fully; this gives a springy texture to the buns.
  Serve the buns while still warm from the oven. Any left over can be split and lightly toasted the next day.

● 235 calories/975 kj per portion

148

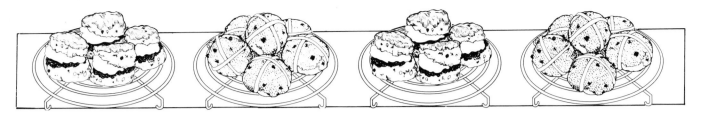

Cherry cloverleaf buns

MAKES 8

 275 g/10 oz packet white bread mix
25 g/1 oz margarine or butter
 75 g/3 oz glacé cherries
! 185 ml/6½ fl oz hand-hot water
vegetable oil, for greasing

ICING
75 g/3 oz icing sugar, sifted
about 1 tablespoon warm water

1 Oil a baking sheet.
2 Put the bread mix into a bowl. Cut the margarine into 1 cm/½ inch cubes and rub in to give a crumbly mixture. Reserve 8 whole cherries; finely chop the remainder, then stir into the bread mixture. Add the water and mix to a dough. Turn out on to a floured surface and knead for 5 minutes.
3 Cut the dough into 8 equal portions, then cut each portion into 3 pieces. Roll each piece into a ball. Take 3 balls and place together on

the baking sheet. Make another group of 3 balls and place on the sheet well apart from the first group.
! Make 6 more groups in the same way.
4 Put 1 whole cherry in the centre of each group. Cover with greased polythene and leave to rise in a warm place for about 1 hour or until doubled in size.
5 Meanwhile, heat the oven to 220C/425F/Gas 7.

6 Uncover the buns and bake in the oven for about 15 minutes until well risen and golden brown. Remove from the oven and place on a wire rack. **✳**
7 Make the icing: mix the icing sugar with just enough warm water to give the consistency of thin cream. Drizzle immediately over the hot buns, then leave on the rack until the buns are cool and the icing is set.

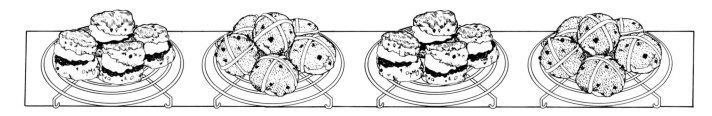

Almond buns

MAKES 12

100 g/4 oz self-raising flour
50 g/2 oz ground almonds
100 g/4 oz margarine or butter,
   softened
100 g/4 oz golden syrup
2-3 drops almond flavouring
2 eggs, lightly beaten
nibbed almonds, to decorate
   (optional)
caster or icing sugar, for
   dusting
vegetable oil, for greasing

1 Heat the oven to 190C/375F/Gas 5.
Brush 12 bun moulds with vegetable
oil (see Cook's tips).
2 Sift the flour into a bowl, then stir
in the ground almonds.

3 In a separate bowl, beat the
margarine until very soft and
creamy. Add the syrup, a little at a
time, beating thoroughly after each
addition. Beat in the flavouring,
then gradually beat in the eggs.
Using a large metal spoon, fold in
the flour and almond mixture.
4 Spoon the mixture into the
prepared bun moulds, dividing it
equally between them, then roughly
level each surface. Lightly sprinkle a
few nibbed almonds on top of each
bun, to decorate, if liked.
5 Bake the buns in the oven for 20-
25 minutes, until well risen, golden
brown and springy to the touch.
Cool the buns for 1-2 minutes, then
remove from the moulds (see Cook's
tips) and place on a wire rack.
Sprinkle with caster sugar and leave
to cool completely.
6 Serve the buns as soon as they are
cold, or store them in an airtight
container (see Storage).

PASTRIES & PIES

Dutch apple tart

SERVES 8

750 g/1½ lb dessert apples
75 g/3 oz seedless raisins
1 teaspoon ground cinnamon
1 tablespoon caster sugar
little beaten egg, for glazing

PASTRY
175 g/6 oz plain flour
pinch of salt
100 g/4 oz butter, softened
75 g/3 oz caster sugar
1 egg

1 Make the pastry: sift the flour and salt into a bowl. Make a well in the centre and add the butter, sugar and egg (see Did you know).
2 Using the fingertips of one hand, gradually work the butter, sugar and egg together, then gradually incorporate the flour until the dough forms a ball. Wrap in cling film and refrigerate for 30 minutes.
3 Heat the oven to 200C/400F/Gas 6.
4 Cut off one-third of the pastry and reserve. Roll out the remaining pastry on a lightly floured surface and use to line a 20 cm/8 inch loose-bottomed flan tin. Trim the edges and reserve the trimmings.
5 Peel, core and cut the apples into 5 mm/¼ inch thick slices. Arrange the slices in the flan case: start at the centre of the flan and arrange the slices overlapping in a spiral shape. Sprinkle over the raisins, cinnamon and sugar.
6 Roll out the remaining pastry and trimmings to make a lattice decoration for the tart (see Preparation). Brush the pastry lattice with beaten egg to glaze.
7 Bake the tart for 20 minutes, then lower the oven to 190C/375F/Gas 5 and bake for a further 15 minutes. Serve hot or cold.

Cook's Notes

TIME
Preparing the tart takes 40 minutes, plus chilling. Cooking takes 35 minutes.

PREPARATION
To make a plain lattice: roll out the reserved pastry to a rectangle, 1 cm/½ inch larger than the diameter of flan tin. Cut into 1 cm/½ inch wide strips. Place half the strips over the flan in parallel lines, then lay the remaining strips in parallel lines across the first set. Trim the edges and press to seal to the flan edge.

DID YOU KNOW
This is a specially rich shortcrust pastry with a higher proportion of butter to flour than usual, extra sugar and a whole egg. This mixture produces a delicate biscuit pastry which, when served cold, retains its crispness and shape.

SERVING IDEAS
Serve with whipped cream sweetened with caster sugar, to taste.

●280 calories/1175 kj per portion

Jam puffs

MAKES 16

**400 g/13 oz frozen puff pastry,
   defrosted**

FILLING
**300 ml/½ pint double or whipping
   cream**
2 teaspoons caster sugar
few drops of vanilla flavouring
about 250 g/9 oz jam
**2-3 tablespoons icing sugar, for
   dredging**

1 Heat the oven to 230C/450F/Gas 8.
Dampen 2 large baking sheets.
2 Roll out the pastry on a lightly
floured surface to a 30 cm/12 inch
square. Trim the edges with a sharp
knife, then cut the square lengthways into 4 equal strips. Cut each
strip across into 4, to make 16
squares (see Cook's tips).
3 Arrange the pastry squares on the
prepared baking sheets, making
sure they do not touch one another.
Bake in the oven (see Cook's tips) for
10-15 minutes, until well risen.
4 Cool the pastries for 2 minutes,
then remove from the baking sheets
and split each square horizontally in
half with a sharp knife. Using your
fingers, pull out and discard any
uncooked pastry. Leave the pastries
on a wire rack to cool completely.
5 Make the filling: whip the cream
with the caster sugar and vanilla
until it forms stiff peaks.
6 To finish: sandwich the pastry
squares back together in pairs,
allowing 1 tablespoon jam and a
generous tablespoon whipped
cream for each square. Sift the icing
sugar over. Serve within 1-2 hours.

TIME
10 minutes preparation,
plus 10-15 minutes bak-
ing. Allow 30 minutes for
cooling and 10 minutes to finish.

COOK'S TIPS
The easiest way to
measure the pastry and
ensure it is cut neatly is to use a
clean plastic ruler. You will find
a ruler helpful in cooking when-
ever accurate sizes are important.
   Place 1 baking sheet in the
centre of the oven and the other
sheet just below it. Swap the
baking sheets and turn them
around after 5 minutes baking
so that the pastries brown
evenly.

WATCHPOINT
Arrange the split
squares side by side in
pairs on the wire rack. The
finished puffs will look untidy if
the wrong halves are put
together when you fill them.

●240 calories/1000 kj per puff

DANISH PASTRIES

BASIC DOUGH
1 teaspoon caster sugar
5 tablespoons warm water
1 tablespoon dried yeast
225 g/8 oz plain flour
25 g/1 oz lard, diced
1 egg, beaten
150 g/5 oz butter, softened and
 divided into 3 equal portions

1 Dissolve the sugar in the water. Sprinkle over yeast and leave for about 10 minutes until frothy.
2 Sift the flour into a warmed large bowl. Rub in the lard, make a well in the centre and pour in the beaten egg and the yeast mixture. Mix to a soft dough.
3 Turn out on to a well-floured surface and knead for about 10 minutes until the dough is smooth. Return the dough to the rinsed-out bowl, cover with cling film and leave for at least 10 minutes.
4 Turn the dough out on to a well-floured surface and roll it into an oblong 10 cm/4 inches wide and 30 cm/12 inches long (it should be 3 times as long as it is wide). Dot 1 portion of butter over the top two-thirds of the dough (see Cook's tip).
5 Fold the fatless third of the dough up to cover the centre third, then fold the top third down to cover it. Press gently with a rolling pin to seal the edges. Wrap in cling film and leave in the refrigerator for 15-20 minutes.
6 Unwrap the pastry and place it on a lightly floured surface so that the folds are to the sides. Roll out and dot with butter as in stage 4, then fold as in stage 5.
7 Repeat stages 4 and 5 once more, making sure that the folded edges of the pastry are always to the sides before you begin to roll.
8 Finally, shape the dough into 6 pin-wheels and 6 half envelopes (see individual recipes).

Pinwheels

MAKES 6
½ quantity basic dough
25 g/1 oz butter
25 g/1 oz caster sugar
1 teaspoon ground cinnamon
40 g/1½ oz sultanas
milk, to seal
vegetable oil, for greasing

TO DECORATE
50 g/2 oz icing sugar, sifted
2 teaspoons warm water

1 Beat butter, sugar and cinnamon together until very pale and fluffy.
2 Roll dough out to a 50 × 10 cm/ 20 × 4 inch strip, and then spread the spice mixture over the dough to cover completely. Scatter evenly with the sultanas. Press down gently so that fruit adheres to mixture.
3 Starting from a short edge, roll up like a Swiss roll. Brush the end with milk and seal, then slice the roll into 6 neat pieces.
4 Heat the oven to 220C/425F/Gas 7 and generously grease a baking sheet with vegetable oil.
5 Place the pastries on the prepared baking sheet, allowing room for expansion, then cover loosely with foil and leave to rise in a warm place for 10-15 minutes until puffed up.
6 Bake for 15 minutes until golden, then leave to cool completely on a wire rack.
7 To decorate: mix the icing sugar with the warm water to make a smooth icing. Using a teaspoon, drizzle the icing in a spiral pattern over the top of each pastry. Or, you can spoon the icing into a greaseproof paper piping bag and pipe over the pinwheel pastries.

Half envelopes

MAKES 6
½ quantity basic dough
3 drained canned apricot halves,
   quartered
vegetable oil, for greasing

CUSTARD
1 tablespoon cornflour
1 tablespoon caster sugar
150 ml/¼ pint milk
few drops vanilla or
   almond flavouring
1 egg yolk

TO DECORATE
1 tablespoon apricot jam
1 teaspoon water
25 g/1 oz flaked almonds, toasted

1 Make the custard: put the corn-flour and the caster sugar in a saucepan and blend them to a smooth paste with a little of the milk. Stir in the rest of the milk until the mixture is well blended.

2 Bring the milk mixture to the boil, stirring constantly, then simmer for 2 minutes until thick. Remove from the heat, allow to cool slightly, then beat in the vanilla and egg yolk. Leave to cool completely.

3 Roll dough out to a 30 × 20 cm/ 12 × 8 inch rectangle, then cut it into six 10 cm/4 inch squares.

4 Place 1 tablespoon of the cold custard in the centre of each pastry square, then arrange a piece of apricot diagonally on either side of the custard. Fold the dough into half envelopes (see Preparation).

5 Heat the oven to 220C/425F/Gas 7 and generously grease a baking sheet with vegetable oil.

6 Place the pastries on the baking sheet, allowing room for expansion, then cover loosely with foil and leave to rise in a warm place for 10-15 minutes until puffed up.

7 Bake for about 15 minutes until golden, then cool completely on a wire rack.

8 To decorate: sieve the jam into a small saucepan, stir in the water and heat through gently. Brush the glaze over the pastries and sprinkle with the toasted flaked almonds.

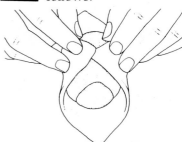

Parisienne choux ring

SERVES 6

175 g/6 oz plain flour
generous pinch of salt
300 ml/½ pint water
100 g/4 oz margarine or butter
4 large eggs, lightly beaten
1 egg, beaten, to glaze
1 tablespoon blanched almonds
1 teaspoon icing sugar
vegetable oil, for greasing

FILLING
6 egg yolks
75 g/3 oz sugar
1 teaspoon vanilla flavouring
65 g/2½ oz plain flour
600 ml/1 pint milk
150 ml/¼ pint double cream,
    thickly whipped

1 Heat the oven to 220C/425F/Gas 7 and lightly grease a baking sheet.
2 Make the pastry: sift the flour and salt on to a sheet of greaseproof paper.
3 Pour the water into a large heavy-based saucepan, add the margarine and heat gently, ☐ stirring occasionally, until the margarine has melted. Bring to the boil, then immediately remove from the heat and tip in the flour.

4 Stir vigorously with a wooden spoon to mix, then return to low heat and beat for about 1 minute, or until the paste forms a ball in the centre of the pan.
5 Remove from the heat and cool for a few minutes, then beat in the eggs, a little at a time. Beat until the paste is smooth and shiny.
6 Put the paste into a piping bag with a 1 cm/½ inch plain nozzle. Pipe a 25 cm/10 inch ring on to the prepared baking sheet. Pipe another ring inside, touching the first ring, then pipe a third ring on top to cover the join.
7 Carefully brush the top of the paste with the beaten egg, then sprinkle with the almonds. Bake in the oven for about 40 minutes.
8 Carefully transfer the choux ring to a wire rack and leave until cold.
9 Meanwhile, make the filling: put the egg yolks in a bowl with the sugar and vanilla, then whisk until pale and thick. Whisk in the flour.
10 Pour the milk into a pan and bring to just below boiling point. Remove from the heat and slowly stir half into the egg mixture. Stir in the remaining milk, then pour back into the pan and whisk constantly over low heat until the mixture thickens and comes to the boil. Remove from the heat and cover closely with a piece of dampened greaseproof paper to prevent a skin forming. Leave until cold.

11 To serve: slice the cold choux ring in half horizontally, then pipe or spoon the filling into the bottom half. Pipe or spoon the whipped cream on top, then replace the upper half of the choux ring. Sift icing sugar over the top and serve.

Cook's Notes

TIME
2 hours to prepare and cook, plus cooling time.

WATCHPOINT
The water must not boil before the margarine has melted, otherwise excess evaporation will affect the balance of ingredients.

SERVING IDEAS
The French like to offer seasonal fruit with, or instead of, dessert.

DID YOU KNOW
This is a version of the classic dessert, Paris-Brest, which is named after a bicycle race that runs in a circle from Paris to Brest (on the coast) and back to Paris. The ring of choux is meant to represent the circular course.

●635 calories/2650 kj per portion

Chocolate orange meringues

SERVES 6

175 g/6 oz plain eating chocolate, broken into pieces

4 tablespoons orange-flavoured liqueur (see Buying guide)

300 g/11 oz can mandarin orange segments, drained

6 meringue nests

150 ml/¼ pint whipping cream

2 tablespoons caster sugar

1 Put the chocolate into a heatproof bowl and add 2 tablespoons of the orange-flavoured liqueur. Set the bowl over a pan of barely simmering water and leave until the chocolate has melted, stirring occasionally.

2 Spear 12 mandarin segments with cocktail sticks. Pat them dry with absorbent paper, then dip them one at a time into melted chocolate to cover completely. Set aside for the chocolate to harden (see Cook's tips).

3 Hold the meringue nests upside down, then dip into the chocolate, leaving the bases uncoated (see Preparation). Set aside on their bases for about 15 minutes until the chocolate has hardened.

4 When ready to assemble, divide the remaining mandarin segments between the meringue shells. Whip the cream until standing in stiff peaks, then fold in the remaining liqueur and the sugar. Spoon the cream over the mandarin segments (see Cook's tips).

5 Remove cocktail sticks from chocolate-coated mandarins and place 2 in the centre of each of the meringue nests. Serve the chocolate orange meringues at once.

Cherry cream slices

MAKES 6 SLICES

400 g/13 oz frozen puff pastry, defrosted

FILLING
425 g/15 oz can stoned black
    cherries in syrup
2 tablespoons cornflour
2 tablespoons water
300 ml/½ pint double cream
3 drops vanilla essence
25 g/1 oz sugar

ICING
225 g/8 oz icing sugar, sifted
2-3 tablespoons warm water
25 g/1 oz dessert chocolate, melted

1 Heat the oven to 230C/450F/Gas 8. Dampen a large baking sheet with water. Cut the pastry in half and roll out each piece to a rectangle, about 30 × 15 cm/12 × 6 inches. Place on the prepared baking sheet and prick well with a fork. Bake in the oven for 15 minutes, turning the pieces round halfway through the cooking time so that they become evenly browned. Transfer to a wire rack and leave to cool completely.
2 Meanwhile, make the filling: place the cherries, with their syrup, in a small saucepan and bring slowly to simmering point. Blend the cornflour to a smooth paste with the water. Remove the pan from the heat and stir in the cornflour mixture. Return to low heat and bring back to the boil, stirring constantly, then set aside to cool completely.
3 Make the icing: blend the icing sugar with enough warm water to give a thick coating consistency.
4 Turn one layer of pastry over and spread the icing over the surface (see Cook's tips).
5 Whip the cream until it begins to thicken; add the vanilla essence and sugar. Continue whipping until the cream stands in stiff peaks.
6 Assemble the dessert: spread the cold cherry mixture over the other layer of pastry, then cover with the whipped cream.
7 Put the iced layer of pastry on top of the cream, iced side up, then lift on to a wooden board and place in the refrigerator for 30 minutes, or the freezer for 20 minutes (see Cook's tips).
8 With a sharp serrated knife, and a sawing motion, carefully cut the pastry into 6 slices. Using a teaspoon, drizzle melted chocolate over the top of each slice in a zig-zag pattern. Return to the refrigerator for 10 minutes to set before serving.

Cook's Notes

TIME
About 4 hours total preparation and cooking time, including cooling the cherry mixture which can take as long as 2 hours.

WATCHPOINTS
When rolling the pastry, keep a good rectangular shape with neat edges.
Before filling, ensure that the cherry mixture and the pastry are well cooled or the cream will melt. To speed up cooling of any mixture, place in a cool container and stand on a wire rack so the air can circulate freely.

COOK'S TIPS
Icing the flat underside of the layer, before turning it over, gives a better finished appearance.
Placing the dessert in the refrigerator or freezer for a short time makes it easier to slice.

STORAGE
Keep covered in a large plastic container in the refrigerator for up to 2 days.

●735 calories/3075 kj per slice

Raspberry and almond tarts

MAKES 18

325-350 g/12 oz shortcrust pastry, defrosted if frozen

FILLING

3 tablespoons raspberry jam
2 egg whites
½ teaspoon almond flavouring
50 g/2 oz caster sugar
15 g/½ oz plain flour, sifted
50 g/2 oz ground almonds
extra caster sugar, to finish

1 Heat the oven to 170C/325F/Gas 3.
2 Roll out the pastry thinly on a lightly floured surface, then cut into as many rounds as possible with a 7.5 cm/3 inch fluted pastry cutter. Knead the trimmings lightly together, roll out and cut into more rounds to make a total of 18.
3 Use the pastry rounds to line 18 tart moulds (see Preparation). Put ½ teaspoon jam into each pastry case.
4 In a clean, dry bowl, whisk the

egg whites until standing in stiff peaks. Whisk in the almond flavouring. Using a large metal spoon, fold in the sugar, flour and ground almonds.
5 Put about 1 heaped teaspoon almond filling into each case, over the jam, then sprinkle lightly with

sugar. Bake in the oven, just above the centre, for about 45 minutes, until the filling is golden brown and firm to the touch.
6 Leave the tarts to cool for a few minutes, until just shrinking from the moulds, then carefully transfer to a wire rack. Leave to cool.

Whirligig pie

SERVES 4-6

400 g/14 oz can apricot halves, drained

500 g/1 lb cooking apples, peeled, quartered, cored and sliced

2 tablespoons sugar

TOPPING
215 g/7½ oz packet puff pastry, defrosted
3 tablespoons caster sugar
1 teaspoon ground cinnamon
extra sugar, for sprinkling

1 Heat the oven to 220C/425F/Gas 7.
2 Arrange the apricots in the base of a shallow 23 cm/9 inch round ovenproof dish. Cover the apricots with the sliced apples, then sprinkle over the sugar. Set them aside.
3 Roll out the pastry very thinly on a lightly floured surface to a large rectangle. Trim the edges straight with a sharp knife, then brush the surface lightly with water. Mix the caster sugar and cinnamon and sprinkle evenly over the pastry.
4 Starting from 1 short side, roll up the pastry like a Swiss roll. Cut across into 5 mm/¼ inch thick slices. ⚠ Arrange the pastry slices over the sliced apples. Sprinkle lightly with sugar.
5 Bake the pie in the oven, above centre, for 35-40 minutes, until the pastry is crisp and golden and the apples feel tender when pierced with a fine skewer. Serve hot or cold (see Serving ideas).

Cook's Notes

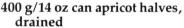

TIME
15 minutes preparation, plus 35-40 minutes baking.

VARIATIONS
Other drained canned fruit can be used instead of the apricots. Omit the cinnamon and mix sugar with grated lemon or orange zest.

WATCHPOINT
Use a sharp knife and cut cleanly; if the pastry is dragged it will not rise well.

SERVING IDEAS
Serve the pie with lightly sweetened soured cream or natural yoghurt.

● 415 calories/1735 kj per portion

Cherry sherry tart

MAKES 6-8 SLICES
150-175 g/6 oz shortcrust pastry,
    defrosted if frozen
lightly beaten egg white, to seal
5 tablespoons redcurrant jelly
4 teaspoons water

FILLING
350 g/12 oz black or red cherries,
    stoned
3 tablespoons custard powder
4 teaspoons sugar
200 ml/7 fl oz milk
1 tablespoon sweet sherry,
    or ¼ teaspoon vanilla flavouring
150 g/5 oz natural yoghurt
150 ml/¼ pint double cream

1 Heat the oven to 200C/400F/Gas 6.
2 Roll out the pastry on a lightly
floured surface and use to line a
loose-based 20 cm/8 inch metal flan
tin. Prick in several places with a
fork. Place a large circle of greaseproof paper or foil in pastry case.
Weight down the paper or foil with
an even layer of baking beans.

3 Bake in the oven for 10 minutes.
Remove paper and beans, brush the
inside of the pastry case with egg
white, then return to the oven for a
further 10-15 minutes, until crisp
and lightly coloured. Remove the
pastry case from tin and leave on a
wire rack to cool completely.
4 Meanwhile, prepare the filling:
mix the custard powder with the
sugar, then blend to a smooth paste
with 1 tablespoon milk. Bring
remaining milk to boil in a small
heavy-based saucepan. Remove
from heat and slowly stir into the
custard mixture. Return mixture to
pan. Bring very slowly to the boil,
stirring, and cook for about 1-2
minutes, until the custard is very
thick and smooth. ⊡
5 Remove from heat and stir in the

sweet sherry. Pour the custard mixture into a bowl, cover closely with
cling film and leave for about 1 hour
to cool completely.
6 Whisk cold custard with a fork.
Gradually whisk in yoghurt, then
continue whisking for 1-2 minutes
more, until smooth. Whip cream
until standing in soft peaks, then
fold it into custard mixture.
7 Put redcurrant jelly and water
into a small heavy-based pan; stir
over low heat until melted. Brush
the inside of the pastry case with a
little of this glaze.
8 Spread the creamy custard
mixture in pastry case. Arrange
cherries on top. Brush remaining
glaze over cherries, then leave for
about 15 minutes to set. Serve the
tart as soon as possible.

Cook's Notes

TIME
Total preparation time
(including cooling time)
is about 2½ hours.

WATCHPOINT
The custard, which is
very thick, must be
thoroughly cooked or it will
taste starchy; take care to keep
the heat low and stir custard
constantly with a wooden
spoon to prevent it 'catching' on
the pan base and scorching.

●360 calories/1500 kj per slice

Harlequin jam tart

SERVES 6

225 g/8-9 oz shortcrust pastry,
  defrosted if frozen

FILLING
2 heaped tablespoons apricot jam
2 heaped tablespoons blackcurrant
  jam
2 heaped tablespoons strawberry
  jam
custard or cream, to serve

1 Heat the oven to 190C/375F/Gas 5.
2 Roll out the pastry on a lightly floured surface and use to line a 23 cm/9 inch ovenproof pie plate. Trim the edges, reserving the trimmings.
3 Using a round-bladed knife, mark the base of the pastry into 6 equal wedges. Spread 1 heaped tablespoon of jam over each wedge, alternating the colours. Refrigerate the tart while you make 3 strips from the pastry trimmings (see Preparation).
4 Place the strips on top of the tart, so that they divide the jam. Dampen the ends of the strips with water, then press on to the pastry edge to seal. Trim the ends, then crimp the edges of the pastry.
5 Bake the tart in the oven, just above the centre, for 30-35 minutes until the pastry is cooked and browned.
6 Serve warm, with custard or cream.

Cook's Notes

 TIME
10 minutes preparation, plus 30-35 minutes baking time.

 FOR CHILDREN
This gaily coloured tart is a winner with children; with some supervision, older children could make it themselves.

 DID YOU KNOW
Harlequin means gaily coloured; the word aptly describes this pretty tart.

PREPARATION
Knead the trimmings lightly together, then roll out to a rectangle measuring 25 × 3 cm/10 × 1¼ inches. Cut lengthways into 3 strips. Gently twist each of them to make a corkscrew shape.

VARIATIONS
You can vary the filling according to the jams and preserves you have in stock, choosing those you think will look most attractive and contrast well with each other.

To ring the changes, use lemon or orange curd, or mincemeat in place of one of the jams.

For harlequin marmalade tart, use orange, lime and dark chunky marmalades instead of the jams.

●275 calories/1150 kj per portion

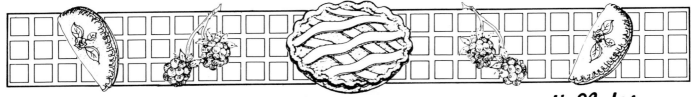

Coffee éclairs

MAKES 8
65 g/2½ oz plain flour, sifted
pinch of salt
150 ml/¼ pint water
50 g/2 oz margarine or butter
2 eggs, beaten

FILLING AND ICING
300 ml/½ pint double cream
coffee icing (see Preparation)

1 Heat the oven to 220C/425F/Gas 7. Line a large baking sheet with foil.
2 Make the choux pastry: sift the flour and salt on to a sheet of greaseproof paper.

3 Put the water and margarine into a heavy-based saucepan and heat gently, stirring occasionally, until the margarine has melted. ⚠ Bring to the boil. Immediately remove from heat and tip in all the flour.
4 Stir vigorously with a wooden spoon to mix, then return to low heat and beat for 1 minute until the paste forms a ball in the centre of the pan. ⚠
5 Remove from heat and cool slightly, then beat in the eggs a little at a time until the paste is smooth and shiny.
6 Put the paste in a piping bag fitted with a 1-2 cm/½-¾ inch star nozzle and pipe 8 éclair shapes on to prepared baking sheet, spacing them well apart.
7 Bake in oven for about 25 minutes until well risen and golden brown.

8 Remove the buns from the oven and slit the side of each bun to allow steam to escape. Return them to the oven and bake for 5 minutes more. Transfer to a wire rack, cut each across in half, then gently scrape out any uncooked mixture from inside. Leave to cool completely.
9 Before serving, whip the cream until stiff, then pipe or spoon into bottom halves. Replace tops.
10 To serve: make coffee icing and spread over éclair tops. Leave in a cool place to set. Serve at once.

Cook's Notes

TIME
1 hour preparation and 30 minutes cooking, plus time for the éclairs to cool and the icing to set.

PREPARATION
To make coffee icing: sift 50 g/2 oz icing sugar into a small bowl, then stir in 1 teaspoon coffee essence and 2 teaspoons warm water. Mix to a smooth paste and use immediately to coat the tops of the éclairs.

SPECIAL OCCASION
For a special occasion, add 1 teaspoon of dark rum to the cream filling before whipping, and continue completing éclairs from the beginning of stage 9.

WATCHPOINTS
The water must not boil before margarine has melted: excess evaporation will upset balance of ingredients.
For the same reason you must remove the pan from the heat as soon as the water is boiling.
Stop beating as soon as the paste forms a ball; otherwise, all the fat will begin to run out and the paste will be unusable.

● 285 calories/1200 kj per portion

Latticed gooseberry tart

SERVES 4

275 g/10 oz shortcrust pastry, defrosted if frozen
little beaten egg, for glazing
caster sugar, for dredging
custard or cream, to serve

FILLING
225 g/8 oz gooseberries, topped and tailed if fresh, defrosted and well drained if frozen
2 tablespoons fresh white breadcrumbs (see Cook's tips)
25 g/1 oz sugar
½ teaspoon finely chopped fresh mint (optional)

1 Heat the oven to 200C/400F/Gas 6.
2 Cut off one-third of the pastry and reserve. On a lightly floured surface, roll out the remaining pastry and use to line a 23 cm/9 inch pie plate.
3 Mix the gooseberries with the breadcrumbs, sugar and mint, if using. Spoon into the pastry-lined pie plate and spread evenly. Brush the edges of the pastry with water.

4 Use the reserved pastry to make a lattice decoration over the tart (see Preparation). Brush the pastry lattice with beaten egg.
5 Bake the tart in the oven, just above the centre, for 20 minutes; then lower the heat to 190C/375F/Gas 5 and bake for about 15 minutes

more, until the gooseberries are tender (see Cook's tips). Cover the top with greaseproof paper if the pastry is browning too quickly.
6 Remove the tart from the oven and sift caster sugar thickly over the top. Serve hot, warm or cold, with custard or cream.

Cook's Notes

 TIME
30 minutes preparation, plus about 35 minutes baking.

 COOK'S TIPS
Breadcrumbs absorb the juices produced by the filling during baking and help prevent the pastry becoming soggy.
Use a fine skewer to test that the gooseberries are tender.

 VARIATIONS
Fresh mint gives a pleasant flavour to gooseberries, but you could use a little grated orange or lemon zest, or ¼ teaspoon ground mixed spice instead.

 PREPARATION
A lattice is a very decorative way of topping a tart. If using a very soft or moist filling, make the lattice on greaseproof paper, then gently shake it on to the tart.
For a scalloped effect, the strips can be cut with a pastry lattice. A plain lattice is made as follows: roll out the pastry to a rectangle, 1 cm/½ inch larger than diameter of the pie plate. Cut in 1 cm/½ inch wide strips. Place half the strips over the tart in parallel lines. Lay the remaining strips in parallel lines across the first set. Trim the edges and press to seal.

●345 calories/1450 kj per portion

Pear pie special

SERVES 4-6

215 g/7½ oz frozen puff pastry, defrosted

FILLING
850 g/1¾ lb firm, dessert pears, quartered and cored
grated zest and juice of 1 orange
25 g/1 oz caster sugar
25 g/1 oz ground almonds
½ teaspoon ground cinnamon
pinch of ground cloves (optional)
little Demerara sugar, to finish

1 Heat the oven to 220C/425F/Gas 7.
2 On a lightly floured surface, roll out the pastry about 4 cm/1½ inches larger all round than the top of a 700 ml/1¼ pint ovenproof pie dish.
3 Cut out a lid and a strip for the rim of the dish from the pastry (see Preparation). Reserve all the pastry trimmings. Leave the pastry in a cool place while making the filling.
4 To make the filling: place the pears in a bowl and sprinkle with the orange zest and juice. Mix well, then turn into the pie dish and arrange over the base. Mix together the caster sugar, ground almonds, cinnamon and cloves, if using, and sprinkle evenly over the pears.
5 Using a pastry brush, dampen the rim of the pie dish. Cut a small piece from the pastry strip (so it will fit neatly), place on the rim of the dish and press down lightly. Brush the strip with water.
6 Place the pastry lid on top of the dish. With your thumb, press the lid and strip together. Using a sharp knife, trim the edges, then knock up and flute them. Make a small thimble-sized hole in the centre of the pastry lid to allow the steam to escape during baking.
7 Roll out the pastry trimmings and use to make leaves or other decorations. Brush the underside of the decorations with water and arrange them on the pastry lid.
8 Brush the lid with water ⚠, then sprinkle lightly with Demerara sugar. Bake in the oven, just above the centre, for 30-35 minutes until the pastry is golden. Serve the pie hot or warm.

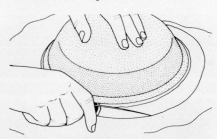

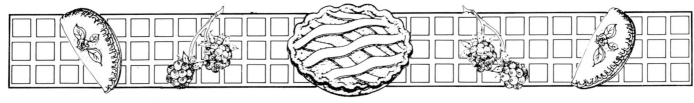

Redcurrant jelly tart

MAKES 10 SLICES

500 g/1 lb redcurrant jelly
150 g/5 oz butter, softened
150 g/5 oz caster sugar
few drops of vanilla flavouring
1 egg, lightly beaten
100 g/4 oz ground almonds
175 g/6 oz plain flour, sifted
icing sugar, for dredging (optional)
lightly whipped cream, to serve
extra softened butter, for greasing

1 Heat the oven to 180C/350F/Gas 4.
Butter a 20 cm/8 inch springform
cake tin (see Cook's tips).
2 Beat the butter and caster sugar
together until very pale and fluffy,
then beat in the vanilla. Add the
egg, a little at a time, beating
thoroughly after each addition.
Using a wooden spoon, gradually
work in the almonds and flour.

3 Draw the mixture into a ball with
your fingers, turn out on to a lightly
floured surface and knead briefly
until smooth (see Cook's tips).
4 Reserve one-quarter of the dough
in a cool place. With your hand,
gently press the remaining dough
over the base and 4 cm/1½ inches of
the way up the sides of the prepared
tin. Neaten the edges.
5 Spread the jelly evenly in the
pastry case.
6 On a lightly floured surface, roll
out the reserved dough to a 22×
5 cm/8½×2 inch strip. Trim edges
with a sharp knife, then cut
lengthways into 6 narrow strips.
7 Dampen the ends of the pastry
strips, then arrange over the jelly in
a lattice pattern. Press the ends
against the pastry edge to seal, then
flute the rim of the pastry. Bake in
the oven for 45 minutes, or until the
pastry is cooked and browned.
8 Sift icing sugar over the top of the
hot tart, if liked. Leave to cool
completely, then remove from the
tin and transfer to a serving plate.

Cook's Notes

TIME
1 hour to make and
bake, plus cooling.

COOK'S TIPS
If you do not have a
springform tin, use a
loose-based sandwich tin.
The dough is very soft; you
may want to flour your hands
when pressing it in the tin.

VARIATIONS
Use bramble, black-
currant or raspberry jelly
in place of redcurrant.

ECONOMY
Replace the jelly with
seedless raspberry jam.
You can reduce the jelly to
225 g/8 oz, but this will give a
thinner filling.

● 465 calories/1950 kj per slice

Butterscotch slice

MAKES 4 SLICES
215 g/7½ oz frozen puff pastry, defrosted

BUTTERSCOTCH FILLING
25 g/1 oz custard powder
300 ml/½ pint warm milk
25 g/1 oz butter
25 g/1 oz dark soft brown sugar
1 tablespoon golden syrup

ICING
50 g/2 oz light soft brown sugar
2-2½ tablespoons water
75 g/3 oz icing sugar, sifted
15-25 g/½-1 oz flaked or chopped almonds, toasted, to decorate

1 Heat the oven to 220C/425F/Gas 7. Dampen a large baking sheet.
2 On a lightly floured surface, roll out the pastry to a 38 × 23 cm/15 × 9 inch rectangle. Trim edges, then cut across into 3 equal strips, each 23 × 12.5 cm/9 × 5 inches.
3 Place the strips on prepared baking sheet and prick well with a fork. Bake in the oven for 10-15 minutes, until risen and golden. Turn strips over and bake 3-5 minutes more to crisp the base. Place on a wire rack and leave to cool completely.
4 Meanwhile, make filling: blend custard powder with a little milk.
5 Put butter, sugar and syrup into a heavy-based saucepan and stir over low heat until melted. Bring to the boil, without stirring, and boil rapidly for 1-2 minutes until deep brown in colour. [!] Remove from heat and pour in remaining milk. [!]
6 Bring mixture slowly to the boil, stirring constantly to ensure butterscotch is completely dissolved. Stir a little of the butterscotch milk into the custard, then return this mixture to pan and bring back to the boil, stirring constantly. Pour into a bowl, cover closely and leave to cool completely.
7 Sandwich pastry layers together with the butterscotch filling.
8 Make the icing: bring the sugar and 1 tablespoon water to the boil. Pour immediately on to icing sugar and mix well, adding the remaining water, if necessary, to give a coating consistency.
9 Spread the icing over top of the pastry slice and decorate with almonds. Leave for about 30 minutes until set before cutting. Serve on the day of making.

Cook's Notes

TIME
Total preparation time is about 2 hours.

WATCHPOINTS
Watch the butterscotch constantly as it can easily overcook and burn.
Stand well back as the milk will splutter fiercely for a few seconds.

● 530 calories/2200 kj per slice

Meringued mince pies

MAKES 8

8 × 6.5 cm/2½ inch vol-au-vent cases, frozen
1 medium egg, separated
6 tablespoons mincemeat
50 g/2 oz caster sugar

1 Heat the oven to 220C/425F/Gas 7.
2 Place the frozen vol-au-vent cases on a dampened baking sheet. Beat the egg yolk and brush the vol-au-vents with a little of it.
3 Put the mincemeat into a small ovenproof dish and cover it tightly.
4 Bake the pastry cases on the centre shelf of the oven and the mincemeat on the bottom shelf for 10-15 minutes, or until the

pastry is risen and golden brown.
5 No more than 5 minutes before the vol-au-vents are cooked, whisk the egg white until very stiff. Gently fold in the sugar with a metal spoon until it is evenly distributed.
6 When the pastry is ready, remove from the oven, together with the heated mincemeat. Keeping the vol-au-vents on the baking sheet, remove the pastry top of each, then use a teaspoon to remove any uncooked pastry. Discard.
7 Fill the vol-au-vents with the mincemeat, then cover each case with meringue mixture. Pile it up into a peak so that the edges are well sealed against the pastry and the mincemeat filling is completely covered.
8 Return the baking sheet to the oven and bake for a further 5 minutes to brown the meringue. Serve hot or cold.

Cook's Notes

 TIME
25-30 minutes to prepare and cook.

 COOK'S TIPS
Always cook puff pastry on a dampened baking sheet. The moisture from the sheet helps to puff up the pastry cases.

 SPECIAL OCCASION
Drain any liquid from the mincemeat and add 1 tablespoon brandy before putting it into the oven. Or buy a high-quality mincemeat that contains little liquid and add the same quantity of brandy to it.

● 135 calories/550 kj per pie

Apple and quince pie

SERVES 4-6

100 g/4 oz plain flour
½ teaspoon ground coriander
pinch of salt
50 g/2 oz butter
1 tablespoon icing sugar
1 egg yolk
1 teaspoon orange juice
1 tablespoon water
milk, for glazing

FILLING
500 g/1 lb cooking apples, peeled
   and cored
350 g/12 oz quinces, peeled and
   cored (see Did you know)
1 teaspoon lemon juice
75 g/3 oz light soft brown sugar
grated zest and juice of 1 orange
2 tablespoons water
15 g/½ oz butter

1 Make the filling: stir the lemon juice into a bowl of water, then slice the apples and quinces into the water to prevent them discolouring.
2 Put the brown sugar in a frying-pan, together with the orange zest and juice and the water. Heat very

Cook's Notes

TIME
About 1¼ hours to make filling and pastry; then 35 minutes for cooking.

DID YOU KNOW
Quinces are related to apples and originally came from Central Asia. Like apples, they are a tree fruit, but have a pronounced 'furry' bloom on their skin. They are not at their best until they turn bright yellow, when their heavy scent is an indication that they are ripe. If quinces are not easy to obtain, use cooking pears in this recipe, with the apples.

●380 calories/1575 kj per portion

gently until sugar has dissolved, then bring to the boil, stirring. Remove from the heat.
3 Drain the apple and quince slices, then add to the pan and stir well. Bring to the boil, then simmer for just 3 minutes. Leave to cool.
4 Meanwhile, make the pastry: sift the flour, ground coriander and salt into a large bowl. Add the butter and rub it in until the mixture resembles fine breadcrumbs. Stir in the sugar. Beat together the egg yolk, orange juice and water, add to flour, then mix to a dough. Wrap and refrigerate for 30 minutes.
5 Heat the oven to 200C/400F/Gas 6.
6 Roll out the pastry on a lightly floured surface to a shape 2.5 cm/1 inch larger all round than the top of a 1.25 L/2 pint ovenproof pie

dish. Invert the pie dish on the rolled-out pastry and cut round the edge with a sharp knife to make a lid. Cut a strip the same width as rim of pie dish, from outer edge of the pastry. Reserve trimmings.
7 Turn the cooled fruit into the pie dish; place a pie funnel in centre.
8 Brush the rim of the dish with water, then press the strip all around the rim. Brush the strip with a little more water, then place the pastry lid on top. Trim the edge of the pastry, then knock up and flute.
9 Make decorations from trimmings, brush the undersides with water and press on to the pastry lid. Brush the lid with milk.
10 Bake pie in oven for 10 minutes, lower heat to 190C/375F/Gas 5 and then bake for a further 25 minutes.

Banana choux buns

MAKES 6

75 g/3 oz plain flour
pinch of salt
150 ml/¼ pint water
50 g/2 oz margarine or butter
2 large eggs, lightly beaten

FILLING

4 teaspoons custard powder
2 tablespoons sugar
300 ml/½ pint milk
150 ml/¼ pint double cream
½ teaspoon vanilla flavouring
2 large bananas

TOPPING

50 g/2 oz plain dessert chocolate,
    broken into pieces
2 tablespoons cold water
25 g/1 oz margarine

1 Make the custard: mix the custard powder with the sugar, then blend smoothly with 2-3 tablespoons milk. Bring the remaining milk to the boil in a saucepan, remove from the heat and stir gradually into the custard mixture.

2 Return to the pan, bring slowly to the boil, stirring constantly, then cook for 1-2 minutes until the custard is smooth and thickened. Pour into a bowl, cover the surface closely with cling film and leave to cool, then chill (see Storage).

3 Heat the oven to 220C/425F/Gas 7. Line a large baking sheet with foil (see Cook's tips).

4 Make the choux pastry: sift the flour and salt on to a sheet of grease-proof paper (see Cook's tips).

5 Put the water and margarine into a large heavy-based saucepan and heat gently, stirring occasionally, until the margarine has melted. ! Bring to the boil, then immediately remove from the heat and tip in all the flour.

6 Stir vigorously with a wooden spoon to mix, then return to low heat and beat for about 1 minute, or until the paste forms a ball in the centre of the pan. !

7 Remove from the heat and cool for a few minutes, ! then beat in the eggs a little at a time, using the spoon or a hand-held electric whisk. Beat for a few minutes more until the paste has a smooth and shiny surface (see Storage).

8 Put the paste into a piping bag fitted with a 2 cm/¾ inch nozzle and pipe 6 rounds on to the prepared baking sheet. (Space well apart to allow for expansion.) Or, put the mixture on to the sheet in 6 mounds using 2 large metal spoons. ✳

9 Bake buns in oven for 25-30 minutes, until well risen and golden brown. Remove from oven and pierce the side of each bun with a sharp knife to allow steam to escape, then bake for 5 minutes more.

10 Transfer the buns to a wire rack. Cut each one across in half, then gently scrape out any uncooked mixture from the inside. Leave to cool completely.

11 Whip the cream with the vanilla until just stiff. Whisk the custard until smooth, then fold it into the cream. Spoon half the mixture into the bottom halves of the buns. Peel and slice the bananas and arrange on top. Spoon the remaining mixture over the bananas, then replace the tops of the buns.

12 Make the topping: put the chocolate and water into a heatproof bowl set over a pan half full of gently simmering water. Heat gently, stirring occasionally, until chocolate has melted, then stir in the margarine. Spoon topping over buns, then leave in a cool place for about 20 minutes, or until set. Serve as soon as possible. !

Cook's Notes

TIME
Total preparation time is about 2½ hours.

COOK'S TIPS
Foil is recommended because the baked buns will lift off it cleanly and easily. (If they stick slightly, they should be returned to the oven for a few minutes more.) As an alternative, use non-stick vegetable parchment paper.

Sifting the flour on to greaseproof paper enables you to add it quickly to the mixture all at once. If added slowly the dough will become lumpy.

WATCHPOINTS
The water must not boil before the margarine has melted, or excess evaporation will upset the balance of the ingredients. For the same reason you must remove the pan from the heat as soon as the water is boiling.

Stop beating as soon as the paste forms a ball; if you continue the fat will run out and the paste will be unusable.

If the eggs are added before the paste has cooled sufficiently, or if they are beaten in too quickly, the mixture will curdle. If beating by hand, you may not need all the egg. Watch the consistency of the dough carefully – it should be just stiff enough to hold its shape and drop slowly from the spoon. If it is too runny the buns will spread badly during baking.

Choux pastry stales quickly and should be eaten on the day of baking. Serve the buns before the filling softens the pastry.

STORAGE
The custard will keep in the refrigerator for up to 24 hours.

Prepare the choux pastry up to the end of stage 7, turn into a polythene container, cover and refrigerate up to 24 hours.

FREEZING
Choux pastry is best frozen unbaked: prepare the dough up to the end of stage 8, open freeze then pack in a single layer in a rigid container. Seal, label and return to the freezer for up to 6 months.

To bake: place frozen buns on lined baking sheet and continue from the beginning of stage 9, allowing 5 minutes extra cooking time before piercing.

● 410 calories/1700 kj per bun

Mile high plum pie

SERVES 6

350 g/12 oz shortcrust pastry, defrosted if frozen
milk and caster sugar, for glazing

FILLING
1 tablespoon cornflour
1 teaspoon ground cinnamon
175 g/6 oz caster sugar
750 g/1½ lb ripe plums (see Buying guide), halved and stoned
pouring cream or custard, to serve

1 Heat the oven to 190C/375F/Gas 5.
2 On a lightly floured surface, roll out just under half of the pastry and use to line a 20 cm/8 inch pie dish.
3 Place the cornflour, cinnamon and sugar in a strong, large polythene bag, then add the plums and shake well until the fruit is coated with the sugar mixture.
4 Turn the plum and sugar mixture into the pastry-lined plate, mounding it slightly in the centre. Brush the pastry edges with water.
5 On a lightly floured surface, roll out the remaining pastry to a 24 cm/9½ inch circle and use to cover the pie. Brush the pastry lid with milk, then sprinkle with caster sugar. Pierce the top with a skewer or fork to make a steam vent.
6 Bake in the oven for about 45 minutes, until the pastry is golden brown. Serve hot or warm.

Cook's Notes

TIME
Preparation takes 20-25 minutes; baking time is about 45 minutes.

VARIATION
Cherry plum pie: use only 350 g/12 oz plums and 75 g/3 oz caster sugar; omit cinnamon and cornflour and mix the sweetened plums with a 400 g/14 oz can commercial cherry pie filling.

BUYING GUIDE
Victoria plums are ideal for this recipe. Other ripe plums can be used, but they must be firm—soft plums do not make a good filling.

●410 calories/1725 kj per portion

Cream horns

MAKES 6

215 g/7½ oz frozen puff pastry,
   defrosted
milk, for brushing
caster sugar, for sprinkling
6 rounded teaspoons strawberry or
   raspberry jam
150 ml/¼ pint double cream
margarine or butter, for greasing

1 Roll out the pastry on a floured
surface to a 50 × 15 cm/20 × 6 inch
rectangle, taking care that you do not
stretch the pastry. Trim the edges
neatly then cut lengthways into 6
strips, 2.5 cm/1 inch wide.
2 Lightly grease 6 cream horn moulds
with margarine or butter. Brush 1
pastry strip with a little cold water
and, with the damp side inwards,
wind it around a greased mould: start
at the pointed end of the mould, and
make sure that the strip overlaps itself
by 5 mm/¼ inch (see Preparation).
Repeat with the remaining strips.

Cook's Notes

TIME
50 minutes preparation,
including standing time
for the pastry, then 20 minutes
baking. Allow for cooling and 5
minutes to fill.

COOK'S TIP
The cooked pastry horns
lose their fresh crispness
very quickly. Start making the
horns just 2 hours before the
party to be sure that they are still
crisp when you serve them, and
fill them at the very last minute
before serving.

PREPARATION
To make the horns from
the pastry strips:

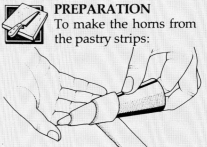

Moisten 1 strip and, with the damp
side facing inwards, wind it around
a greased mould: start at the pointed
end and overlap 5 mm/¼ inch.

● 300 calories/1250 kj per horn

3 Place the horns, with the end of the
strip underneath, on a dampened
baking sheet, and leave to stand for 30
minutes.
4 Heat the oven to 230C/450F/Gas 8.
5 Bake the horns for 15 minutes.
Remove from the oven, brush lightly
with milk and sprinkle with a little
caster sugar, then return to the oven
and bake for a further 3-5 minutes,
until the pastry is golden brown.

6 Transfer to a wire rack and leave to
cool for 5 minutes, then remove the
moulds and leave them to cool
completely.
7 Just before serving, spread 1
heaped teaspoonful of jam around the
inside of each horn. Whip the cream
until standing in soft peaks and use to
fill a piping bag fitted with a large star
nozzle. Pipe into the horns. Serve at
once.

Viennese tarts

MAKES 6
100 g/4 oz plain flour
25 g/1 oz cornflour
100 g/4 oz butter or margarine, at room temperature
25 g/1 oz icing sugar
3 drops vanilla flavouring

TO FINISH
icing sugar, for dredging
1 tablespoon redcurrant jelly or seedless raspberry jam (see Cook's tip)

1 Heat the oven to 180C/350F/Gas 4. Line each mould of a 6-mould tart tin with a paper case.

2 Sift the flour and cornflour into a bowl and set aside.

3 Put the butter in a separate bowl, then sift in the icing sugar. Beat until pale and fluffy, then beat in the vanilla. Beat in about one-quarter of the flour mixture until evenly incorporated. Add the remaining flour mixture in the same way.

4 Put the mixture into a piping bag fitted with a large star nozzle and pipe it into the paper cases (see Preparation). Bake in the oven for 20-25 minutes, until set and lightly browned.

5 Cool the tarts for 10 minutes, then carefully lift them out of the moulds (still in their paper cases) and leave on a wire rack to cool completely.

6 To finish: sift icing sugar generously over the top of each tart, then put about ½ teaspoon redcurrant jelly into the centre.

Cook's Notes

TIME
25 minutes preparation and 20-25 minutes baking. Cooling takes about 30 minutes. Allow a few more minutes for finishing.

COOK'S TIP
If you do not have redcurrant jelly or seedless raspberry jam, simply sieve any red jam.

STORAGE
These tarts will keep for up to 1 week in an airtight container.

PREPARATION
To pipe the mixture into the paper cases:

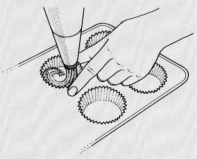

Hold the case steady with one hand. Starting at the centre of the base of the case, pipe the mixture in a spiral around the sides of the case to leave a shallow hollow in the top.

●230 calories/950 kj per tart

Coconut tartlets

MAKES 16

 225 g/8-9 oz shortcrust pastry,
    defrosted if frozen

 3 tablespoons apricot jam
50 g/2 oz margarine or butter
50 g/2 oz caster sugar
1 egg, beaten
50 g/2 oz desiccated coconut
3 tablespoons self-raising flour
a little milk (optional)

TO DECORATE
75 g/3 oz icing sugar
3 tablespoons toasted desiccated
    coconut (see Preparation)

1 Heat the oven to 190C/375F/Gas 5.
2 Roll out the pastry thinly on a lightly floured surface. With a 6.5 cm/2½ inch fluted or plain pastry cutter, cut out 16 rounds. Line 16 tartlet tins with the pastry rounds, then spoon a little apricot jam into each one.
3 Beat together the margarine and sugar until light and fluffy, then gradually beat in the egg. Using a large metal spoon, fold in the coconut and flour and add a little milk, if necessary, to give a soft, dropping consistency.
4 Divide the coconut mixture equally between the tins. Bake in the oven for 15-20 minutes until the coconut mixture is golden brown and just firm to the touch. Carefully ease the tartlets out of the tins and leave to cool on a wire rack.
5 When the tartlets are cold, make the decoration: sift the icing sugar into a bowl and stir in a little warm water to give a smooth icing that coats the back of the spoon. With a teaspoon, put a little icing on each tartlet and sprinkle the toasted coconut on top.

Toffee tarts

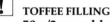
MAKES 12

**225 g/8-9 oz shortcrust pastry,
defrosted if frozen**

TOFFEE FILLING
50 g/2 oz golden syrup
50 g/2 oz caster sugar
50 g/2 oz margarine, diced
40 g/1½ oz glacé cherries, quartered
40 g/1½ oz flaked almonds
40 g/1½ oz sultanas

1 Heat the oven to 200C/400F/Gas 6.
2 Roll out the pastry thinly on a lightly floured surface, then cut into as many rounds as possible with a 7.5 cm/3 inch fluted pastry cutter. Knead the trimmings lightly together, roll out and cut into more rounds to make a total of 12.
3 Use the pastry rounds to line 12

tart moulds. Prick base and sides of each pastry case with a fork, then bake in oven for about 12 minutes or until crisp and golden. Cool for 2-3 minutes, then carefully remove from moulds and leave on a wire rack to cool completely.
4 Meanwhile, make the filling: put the syrup, sugar and margarine into a saucepan and stir over low heat until the margarine has melted and

sugar has dissolved. Bring slowly to the boil, without stirring, and boil for 2 minutes. [!] Remove from the heat and stir in the cherries, almonds and sultanas.
5 Leave the mixture to cool and thicken for 10 minutes, then divide equally between the pastry cases. Leave for about 30 minutes or until the toffee tarts are completely cold before serving (see Storage).

Apple and sultana tartlets

MAKES 15
RICH SHORTCRUST PASTRY
200 g/7 oz plain flour
pinch of salt
2 tablespoons icing sugar
1 egg, separated
100 g/4 oz butter, softened

FILLING
1 cooking apple, about 175 g/6 oz
75 g/3 oz sultanas
1 teaspoon ground cinnamon
2 tablespoons soft brown sugar

1 Heat the oven to 200C/400F/Gas 6.
2 To make the pastry: sift the flour and salt on to a work top and sift on the icing sugar. Make a well in the centre and put in the egg yolk and butter. With your fingertips, gradually work in flour from the edges until a smooth ball of dough is formed. Cover it with a clean tea-towel and leave it to relax while you prepare the filling.
3 Peel, core and very finely chop the apple and mix it in a bowl with the sultanas, cinnamon and sugar.
4 Roll out the pastry and stamp out equal numbers of 6.5 cm/2½ inch and 5 cm/2 inch rounds. Using an apple corer or a very small pastry cutter stamp out a small round in the centre of each 5 cm/2 inch circle. Use the trimmings to make more circles in the same way.
5 Line small, floured tartlet tins with the large circles. Put a pile of apple mixture into each, moisten the edges with water and cover with a small holed circle. Gently press down the edges, making slightly raised volcano shapes.
6 Brush the tartlets with the egg white and bake them for 15-20 minutes or until golden brown.
7 Serve hot for dessert with cream, or leave to cool on wire racks.

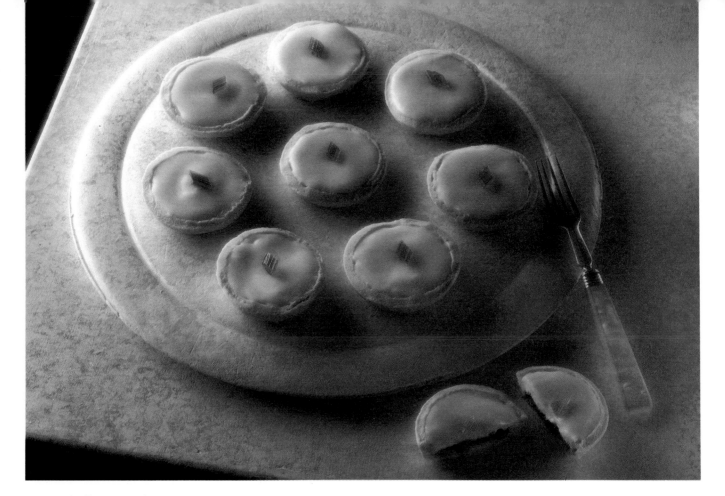

Cranberry cream tartlets

MAKES 9 TARTLETS
100 g/4 oz plain flour
pinch of salt
65 g/2½ oz butter, diced
15 g/½ oz caster sugar

FILLING AND ICING
185 g/6½ oz jar cranberry sauce (see Cook's tip)
150 ml/¼ pint double cream, whipped
75 g/3 oz icing sugar
2-3 teaspoons lemon juice
few drops of cochineal food colouring
small strip of angelica, cut into leaf shapes, to decorate

1 Heat the oven to 200C/400F/Gas 6.
2 Make the pastry: sift the flour and salt into a bowl, add the butter and rub in until the mixture resembles fine breadcrumbs. Stir in sugar, then add enough water to bind mixture together to a firm but pliable dough.
3 Roll the pastry out thinly on a lightly floured surface, then cut into 9 rounds with a 7.5 cm/3 inch pastry cutter. Use to line 9 deep individual tartlet tins, then prick the bases with a fork.
4 Bake just above the centre of the oven for about 15 minutes, or until the pastry is cooked through and pale golden in colour. Cool the pastry cases for 2-3 minutes, then carefully remove from the tins, place on a wire rack, and leave to cool completely.
5 To fill tartlets: put 1 teaspoon of cranberry sauce in the base of each pastry case, then top with a teaspoon of whipped cream. Smooth the surface so that it is level with the top of the pastry.
6 Blend the icing sugar with the lemon juice to form a thick, smooth icing, then add a few drops of cochineal to give the icing a very delicate pink colour. [!]
7 Carefully spoon a little icing over each tartlet and spread lightly with a knife until it completely covers the cream. [!] Refrigerate for 1 hour.
8 Decorate with small leaves of angelica. Serve the same day.

Cook's Notes

TIME
30 minutes to make the pastry cases, plus the cooling time; 20 minutes to fill and ice, then 1 hour chilling.

WATCHPOINTS
Be very careful with the cochineal, making sure to use only a few drops – bright pink icing looks unappetizing.
Take care not to mix the cream into icing; they should remain in 2 separate layers.

COOK'S TIP
If the cranberry sauce seems to be runny, drain it before use, then stir well – this will avoid making the pastry soggy.

STORAGE
The pastry cases can be made in advance and stored in an airtight tin for up to 2 days, if liked.

●255 calories/1075 kj per tartlet

Plum tartlets

MAKES 40
450 g/1 lb plain flour
pinch of salt
225 g/8 oz margarine or butter
50 g/2 oz caster sugar
water, to bind

FILLING
3 tablespoons plum jam
20 large plums, halved and stoned
50 g/2 oz Demerara sugar
300 ml/½ pint double cream
50 g/2 oz plain dessert chocolate
   (see Watchpoint)

1 Sift the flour and salt into a bowl. Cut the margarine into 1 cm/½ inch cubes, add to the flour and rub in until the mixture resembles fine crumbs. Add the sugar, mix lightly, then sprinkle in enough water to draw the mixture together into a firm dough.
2 Heat the oven to 200C/400F/Gas 6.

3 Turn the pastry on to a floured surface, knead lightly and roll out. Using a 7.5 cm/3 inch fluted pastry cutter, cut out 40 circles and use to line deep tartlet tins (see Cook's tips). Prick the bases with a fork.
4 Spread about ¼ teaspoon jam over the base of each tartlet case (see Cook's tips). Place half a plum in each case, skin side up, and sprinkle with the sugar.
5 Bake in the oven, for 25-30

minutes or until the plums are just tender and the pastry is crisp and golden.
6 Remove from the oven, transfer the cases to a wire rack and leave until completely cold.
7 Whip the cream until it forms stiff peaks, then spoon or pipe a little on top of each plum. Grate the chocolate coarsely over the cream, then transfer the tarts to a large serving platter and serve.

Cook's Notes

 TIME
30 minutes preparation, 25-30 minutes cooking, plus cooling time.

COOK'S TIPS
If you do not have enough tartlet tins, make the tartlets in batches. Leave the pastry, covered with cling film, in the refrigerator in between baking batches.

Use a stiff pastry brush for spreading the jam.

WATCHPOINT
If the weather is warm, chill the chocolate in the refrigerator for 30 minutes before grating or it may be too soft to grate satisfactorily.

VARIATION
When apricots are in season, use them instead of plums: replace the plum jam with apricot jam.

●140 calories/600 kj per tartlet

Maids of Honour

MAKES 12
215 g/7½ oz frozen puff pastry, defrosted

FILLING
50 g/2 oz cottage cheese
50 g/2 oz caster sugar
2 egg yolks
15 g/½ oz butter, melted
25 g/1 oz ground almonds
2 teaspoons brandy or milk

1 Heat the oven to 200C/400F/Gas 6.
2 On a lightly floured surface, roll out the pastry very thinly and cut into as many rounds as possible with a 9 cm/3½ inch plain cutter. Layer the pastry trimmings on top of each other, roll out thinly and cut into more rounds. **!** You should make 12 altogether.
3 Use the pastry rounds to line 12

tart moulds. Prick pastry bases well in several places with a fork then place the tart tray in the refrigerator while making the filling.
4 Sieve the cheese into a bowl. Using a wooden spoon, work in the sugar, egg yolks and butter. Stir in almonds and brandy, mixing well.

5 Divide the filling equally between the pastry cases (see Cook's tips). Bake the tarts in the oven for about 25 minutes, or until the filling is risen and just firm to the touch.
6 Cool the tarts in the tray for 2-3 minutes, then transfer to a wire rack. Serve warm (see Cook's tips).

Cook's Notes

TIME
30 minutes preparation and 25 minutes baking, plus about 10 minutes cooling.

DID YOU KNOW
These small tarts are thought to date from Henry VIII's time. According to one story the king suggested the name as the tarts were very popular with the Maids of Honour who attended his wives at the palace in Richmond.

● 130 calories/550 kj per tart

WATCHPOINT
Do not knead the trimmings — this destroys the airy texture of the pastry.

COOK'S TIPS
The prepared cases should be only about one-third full as the pastry and filling puff up during baking.

Any left-over tarts can be stored in an airtight container for 1-2 days, then warmed through in a 180C/350F/Gas 4 oven for about 5 minutes just before serving time.

Jap cakes

MAKES 10
2 large egg whites
100 g/4 oz caster sugar
75 g/3 oz ground almonds
50 g/2 oz plain dessert chocolate, melted, to finish

CHOCOLATE BUTTERCREAM
50 g/2 oz icing sugar
2 teaspoons cocoa powder
25 g/1 oz butter, softened
1 teaspoon hot water

Cook's Notes

TIME
Allow 20 minutes, plus baking and cooling for the rounds; filling and finishing (including chilling time) take 35-45 minutes.

STORAGE
The biscuits will keep fresh and crisp for 1-2 days in an airtight container in a cool place. Do not store in the refrigerator as this will make the biscuits lose their crisp texture.

● 150 calories/625 kj per cake

PREPARATION
Dip the biscuit pairs as shown:

Hold the biscuit on its side and dip into the melted chocolate so that one edge is well coated, giving a crescent effect.

1 Heat the oven to 140C/275F/Gas 1. Line 2 baking sheets with non-stick vegetable parchment paper or oiled greaseproof paper.
2 In a clean, dry bowl, whisk the egg whites until standing in stiff peaks. Whisk in the sugar, 1 tablespoon at a time, and continue to whisk until meringue is stiff and glossy. Fold in ground almonds.

3 Put the mixture into a piping bag fitted with a large plain nozzle. Pipe twenty 5 cm/2 inch rounds on to baking sheets, spacing them about 2.5 cm/1 inch apart.
4 Bake below centre of oven for 1-1¼ hours, until firm and crisp. Swap sheets halfway through baking. Peel the paper off the rounds while warm, then cool completely.

5 Make the buttercream: sift icing sugar with the cocoa. Beat butter until very soft, then slowly beat in sugar mixture and water.
6 Sandwich the rounds in pairs with buttercream, then refrigerate for 15-20 minutes to firm.
7 Dip in melted chocolate (see Preparation) and leave on a wire rack to set before serving (see Storage).

INDEX